A Bintel Brief.

A Bintel Brief

Love and Longing in Old New York

Liana Finck

ECCO

AN IMPRINT OF HARPERCOLLINS PUBLISHERS

HARPERCOLLINS BOOKS MAY BE PURCHASED FOR EDUCATIONAL, BUSINESS, OR SALES PROMOTIONAL USE. FOR INFORMATION PLEASE E-MAIL THE SPECIAL MARKETS DEPARTMENT AT SPSALES@HARPERCOLLINS.COM.

FIRST EDITION

PRINTED ON ACID-FREE PAPER

Library of Congress CATALOGING-IN-PUBLICATION DATA HAS BEEN APPLIED FOR.

ISBN 978-0-06-229161-5

14 15 16 17 18 ID/RRD 10 9 8 7 6 5 4 3 2 1

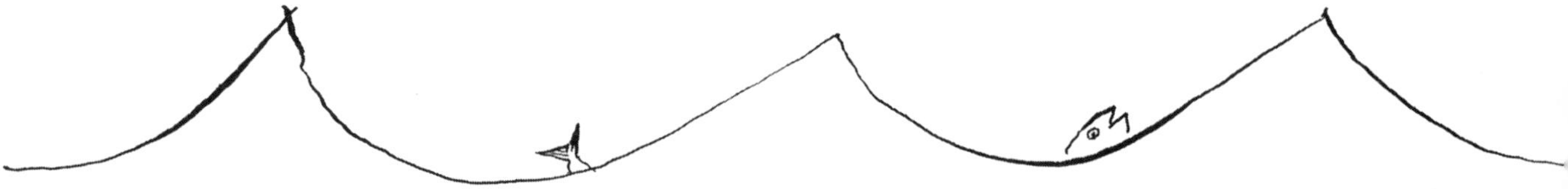

FOR GRANDMA HELEN FINCK,

AND IN MEMORY OF
GRANDMA RO SILBERSTEIN,
PAPA RAYMIE SILBERSTEIN AND
PAPA YANK FINCK

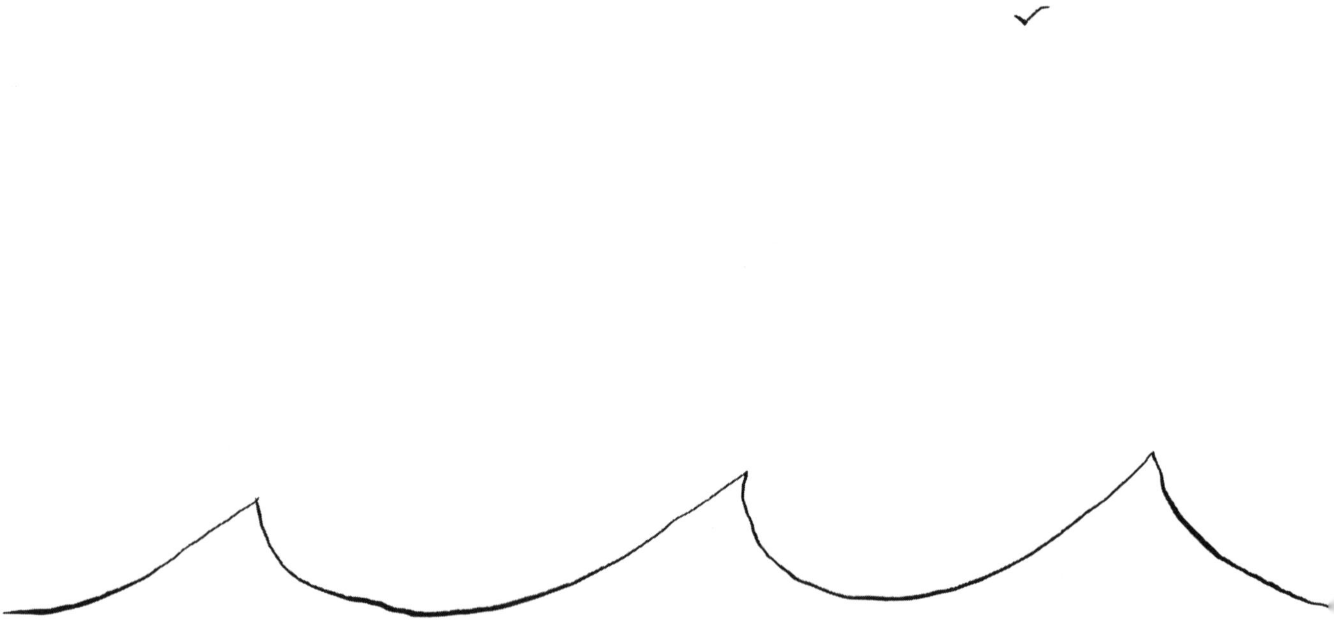

He lived like a small gray grain of sand on the beach, surrounded by millions like him. And when the wind lifted him and transported him across the ocean to the opposite shore, no one noticed.

—I.L. Peretz

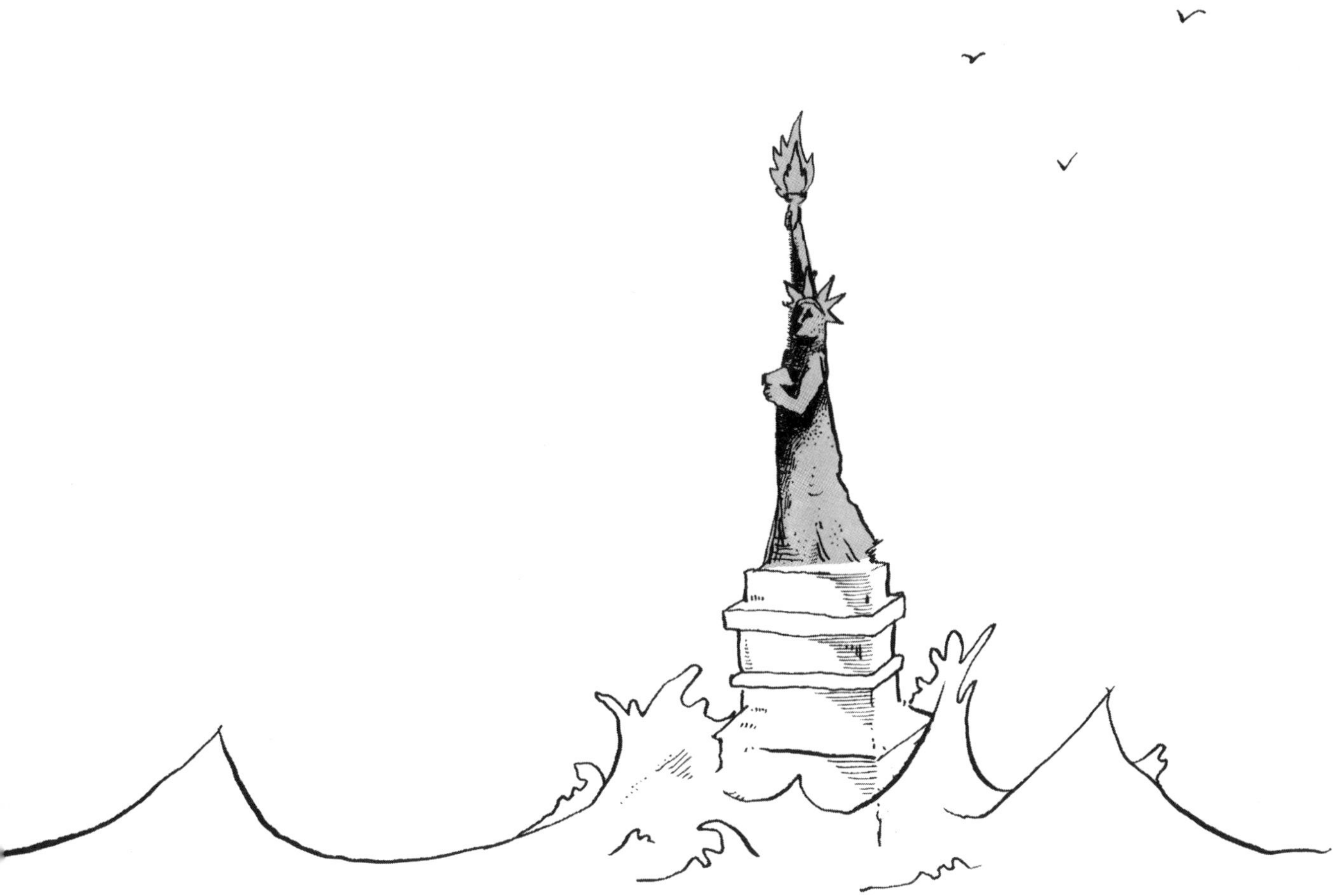

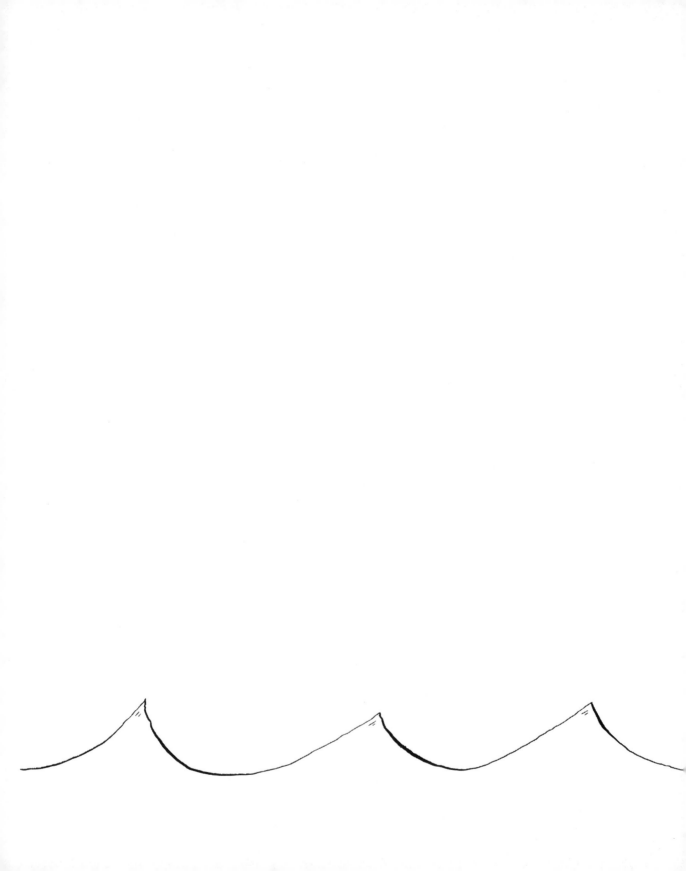

A Bintel Brief

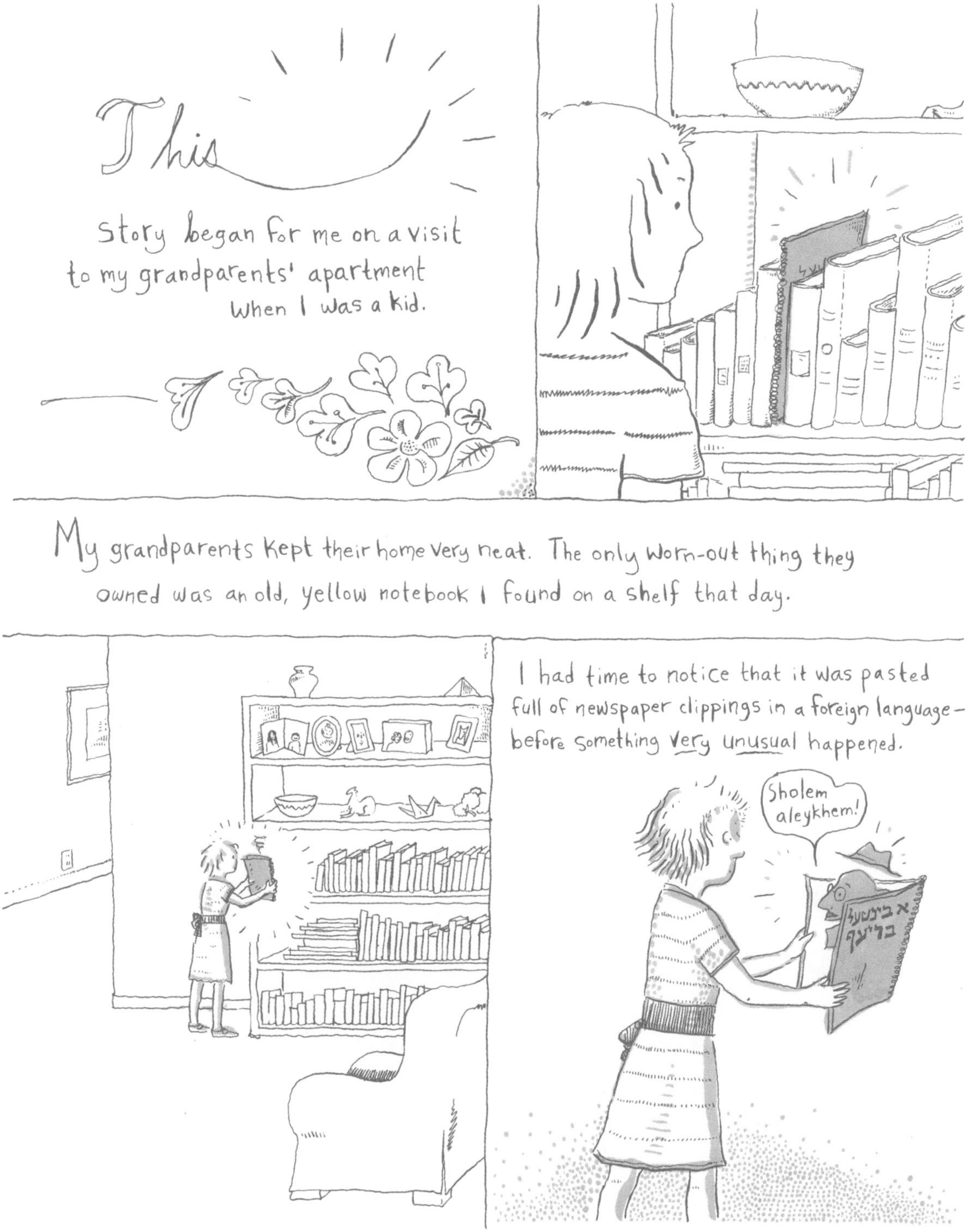
This story began for me on a visit to my grandparents' apartment when I was a kid.
My grandparents kept their home very neat. The only worn-out thing they owned was an old, yellow notebook I found on a shelf that day.
I had time to notice that it was pasted full of newspaper clippings in a foreign language— before something very unusual happened.
Sholem aleykhem!

And that was the last I saw of the Bintel Brief for a long time.

Many years later, I was living in New York. One day, I received a mysterious package in the mail. It was from my grandmother. When I opened it, there was the notebook!

I hid it under a pile of stuff.

("stuff") →

Even so, it was hard to concentrate knowing that the strange, portentous object was nearby.

Finally, I couldn't take the tension anymore.

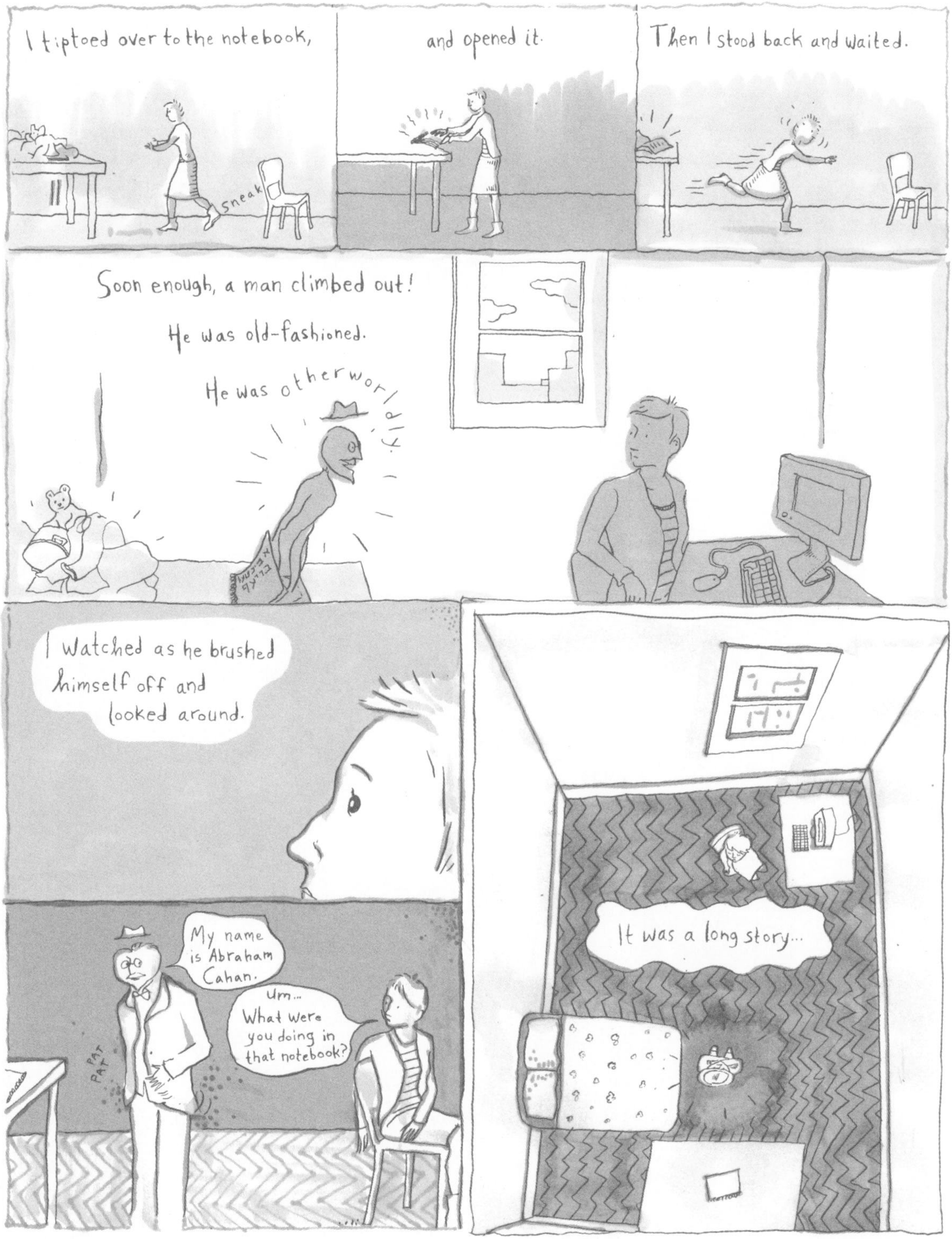
I tiptoed over to the notebook,
sneak
and opened it.
Then I stood back and waited.
Soon enough, a man climbed out!
He was old-fashioned.
He was otherworldly.
I watched as he brushed himself off and looked around.
My name is Abraham Cahan.
PAT PAT
Um... What were you doing in that notebook?
It was a long story...

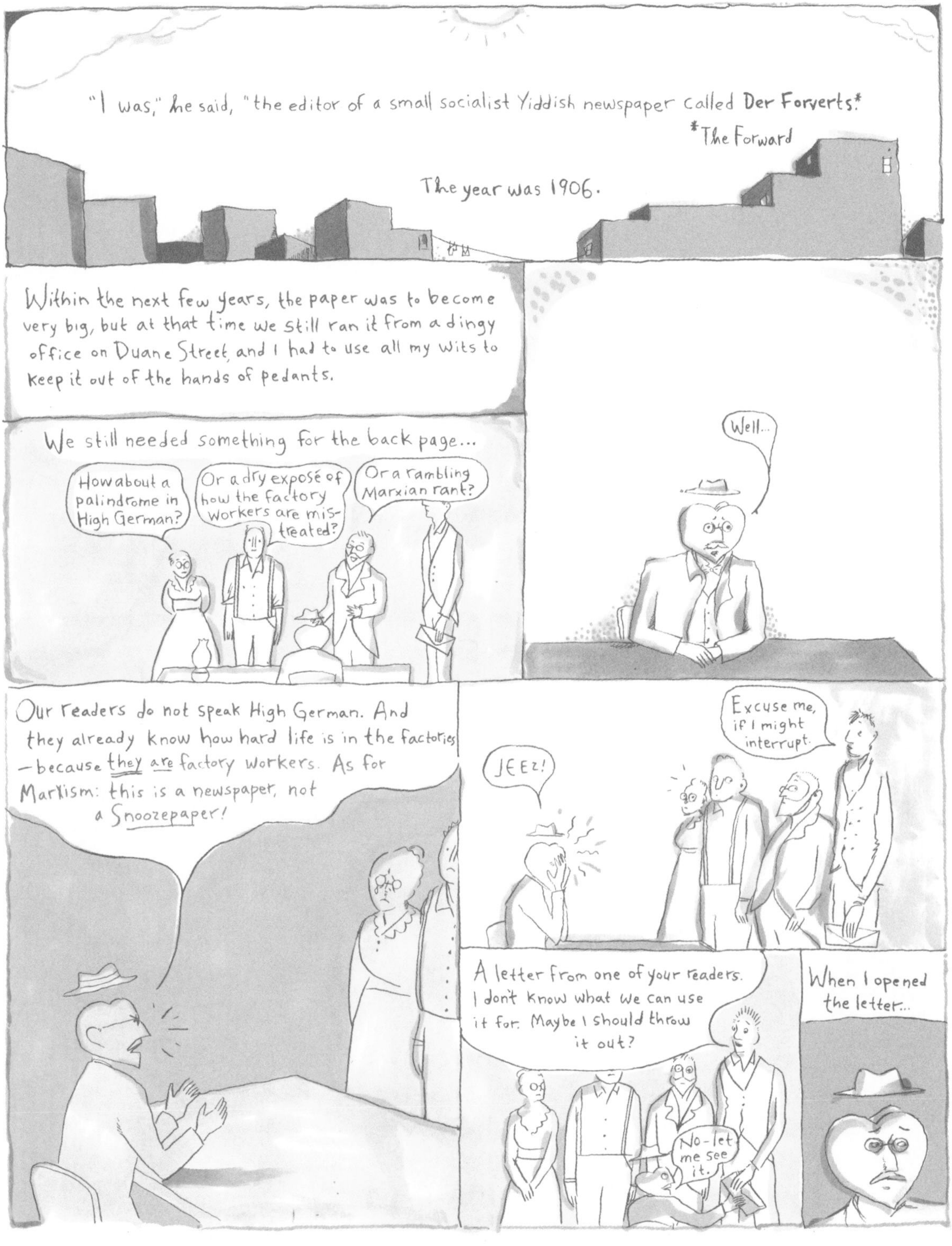
"I was," he said, "the editor of a small socialist Yiddish newspaper called **Der Forverts**.*
*The Forward
The year was 1906.
Within the next few years, the paper was to become very big, but at that time we still ran it from a dingy office on Duane Street, and I had to use all my wits to keep it out of the hands of pedants.
We still needed something for the back page...
How about a palindrome in High German?
Or a dry exposé of how the factory workers are mistreated?
Or a rambling Marxian rant?
Well...
Our readers do not speak High German. And they already know how hard life is in the factories —because they are factory workers. As for Marxism: this is a newspaper, not a Snoozepaper!
JEEZ!
Excuse me, if I might interrupt.
A letter from one of your readers. I don't know what we can use it for. Maybe I should throw it out?
No—let me see it.
When I opened the letter...

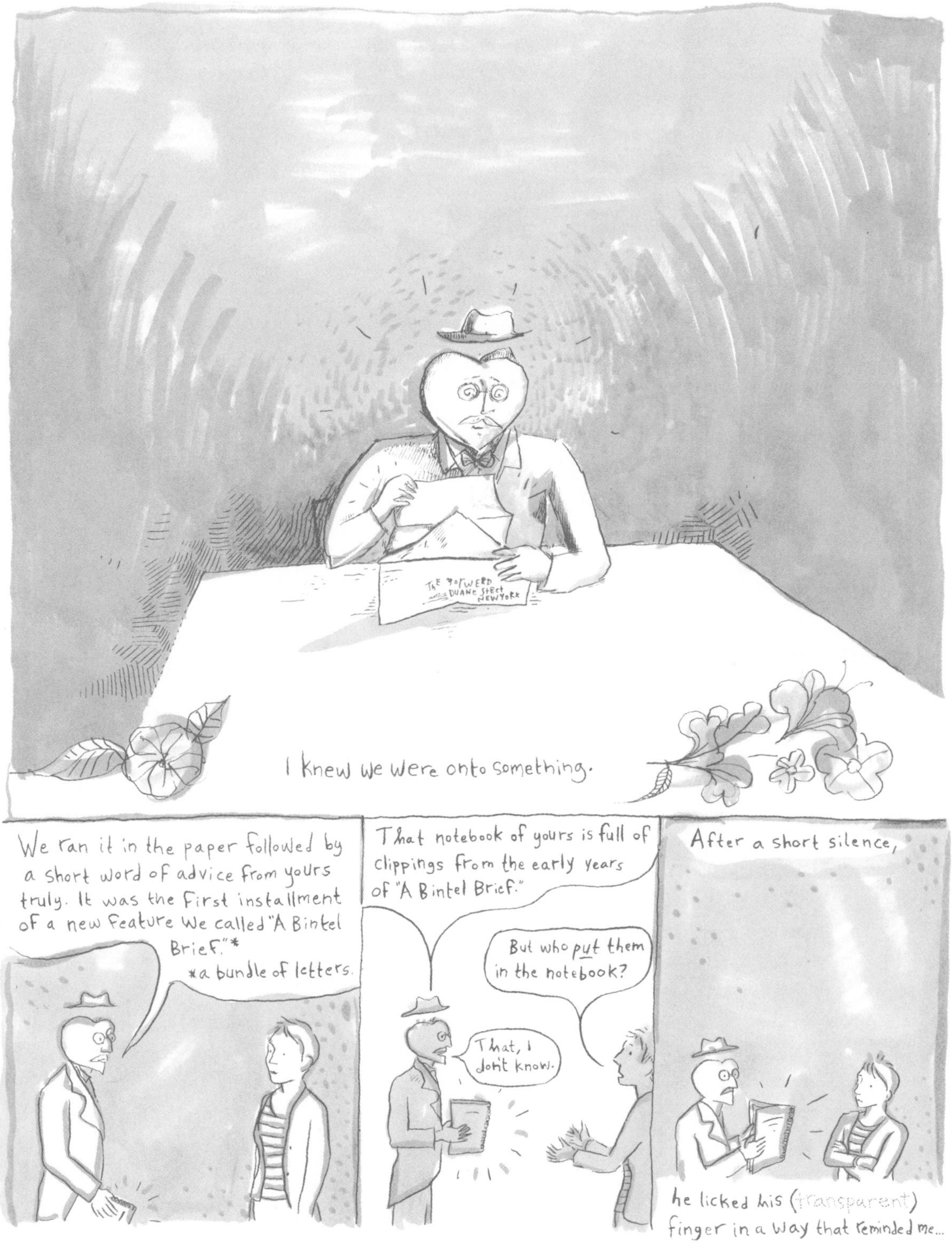
THE FORWERD DUANE STRET NEW YORK
I knew we were onto something.
We ran it in the paper followed by a short word of advice from yours truly. It was the first installment of a new feature we called "A Bintel Brief."*
*a bundle of letters.
That notebook of yours is full of clippings from the early years of "A Bintel Brief."
But who put them in the notebook?
That, I don't know.
After a short silence,
he licked his (transparent) finger in a way that reminded me...

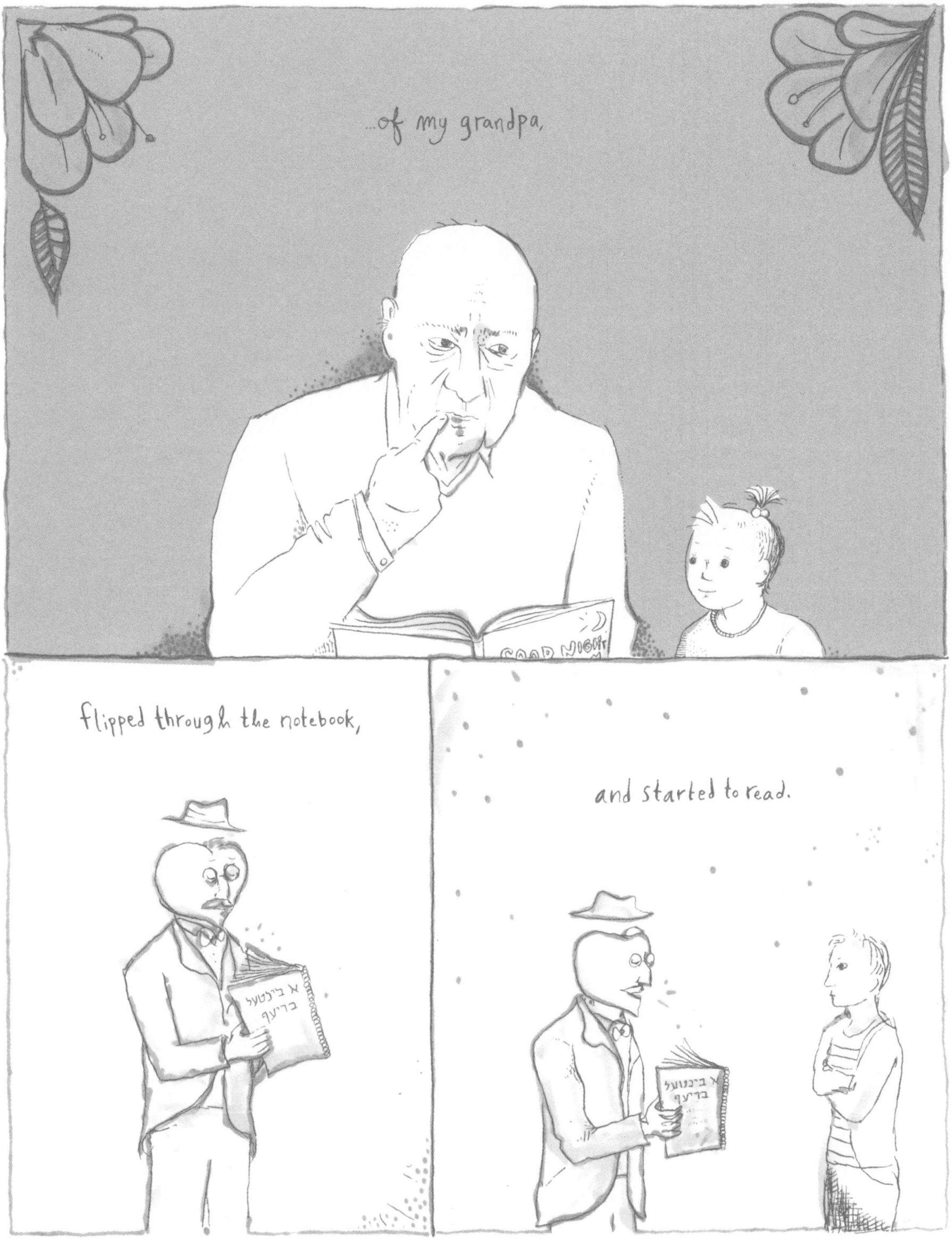
...of my grandpa,
flipped through the notebook,
א בינטעל בריעף
and started to read.
א בינטעל בריעף

1

THE WATCH

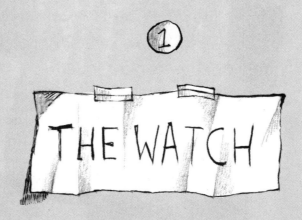

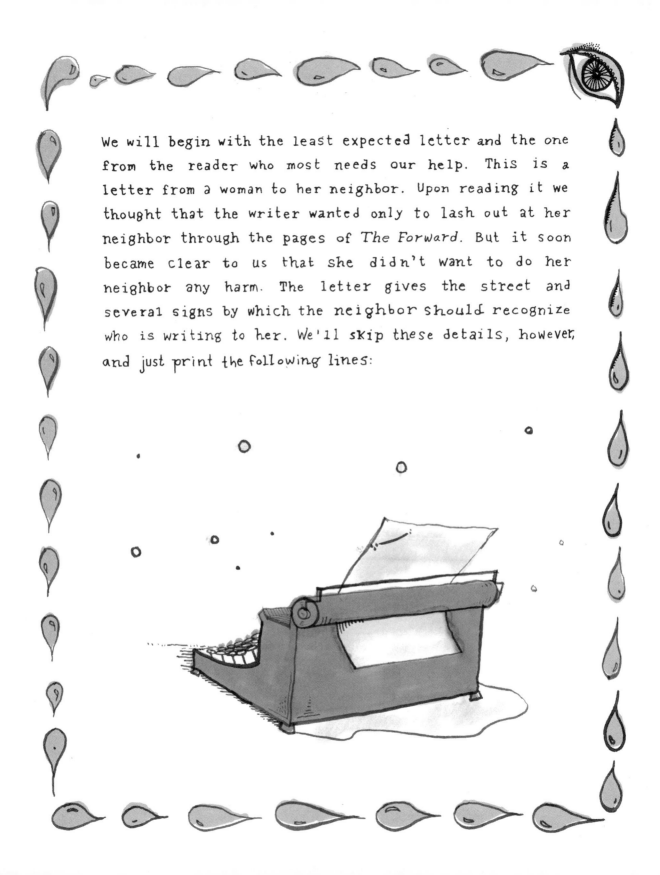

We will begin with the least expected letter and the one from the reader who most needs our help. This is a letter from a woman to her neighbor. Upon reading it we thought that the writer wanted only to lash out at her neighbor through the pages of *The Forward*. But it soon became clear to us that she didn't want to do her neighbor any harm. The letter gives the street and several signs by which the neighbor should recognize who is writing to her. We'll skip these details, however, and just print the following lines:

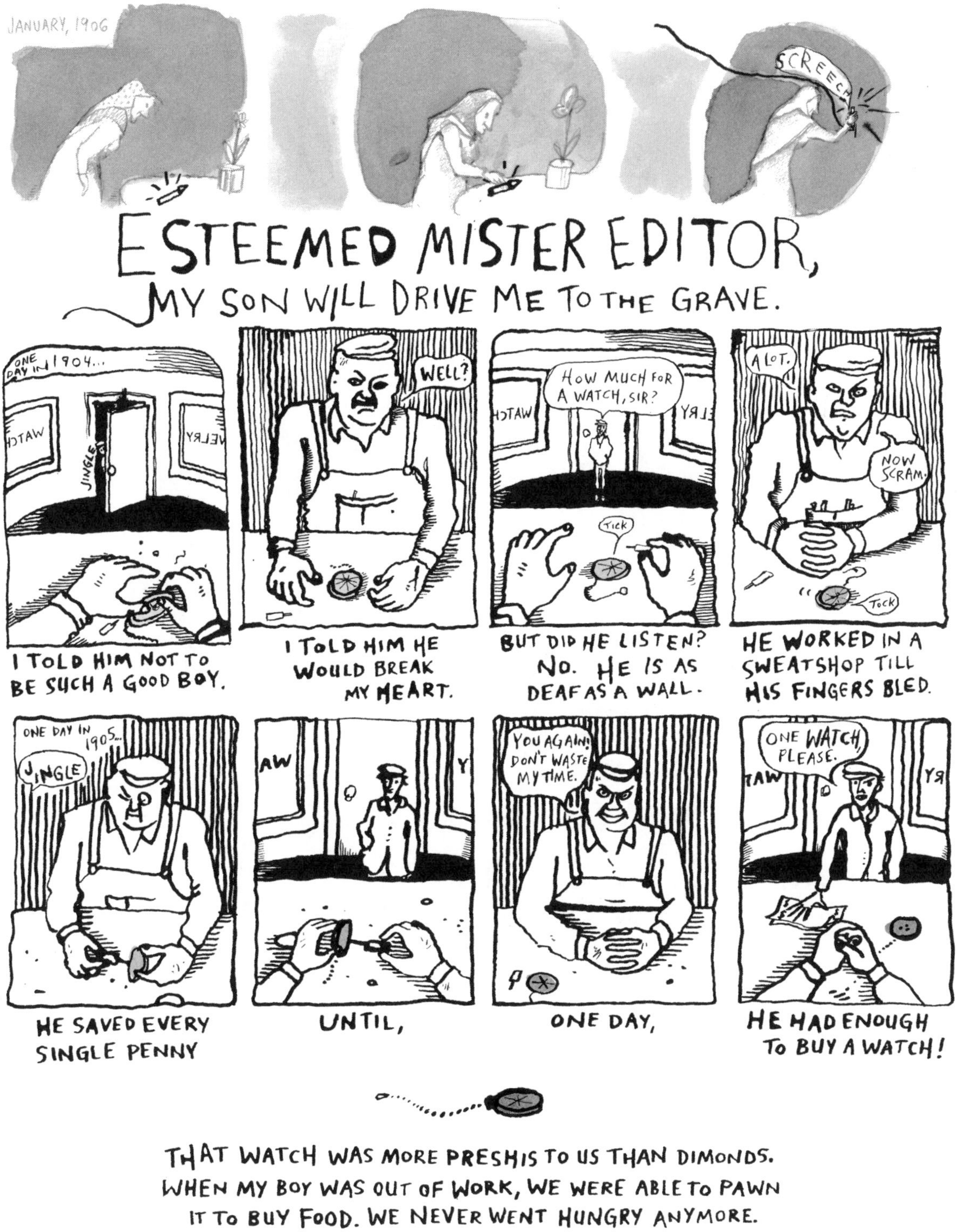

JANUARY, 1906
SCREECH
ESTEEMED MISTER EDITOR,
MY SON WILL DRIVE ME TO THE GRAVE.
ONE DAY IN 1904...
WATCH
VELRY
JINGLE
I TOLD HIM NOT TO BE SUCH A GOOD BOY.
WELL?
I TOLD HIM HE WOULD BREAK MY HEART.
HOW MUCH FOR A WATCH, SIR?
TICK
BUT DID HE LISTEN? NO. HE IS AS DEAF AS A WALL.
A LOT.
NOW SCRAM.
TOCK
HE WORKED IN A SWEATSHOP TILL HIS FINGERS BLED.
ONE DAY IN 1905...
JINGLE
HE SAVED EVERY SINGLE PENNY
UNTIL,
YOU AGAIN! DON'T WASTE MY TIME.
ONE DAY,
ONE WATCH, PLEASE.
HE HAD ENOUGH TO BUY A WATCH!
THAT WATCH WAS MORE PRESHIS TO US THAN DIMONDS.
WHEN MY BOY WAS OUT OF WORK, WE WERE ABLE TO PAWN
IT TO BUY FOOD. WE NEVER WENT HUNGRY ANYMORE.

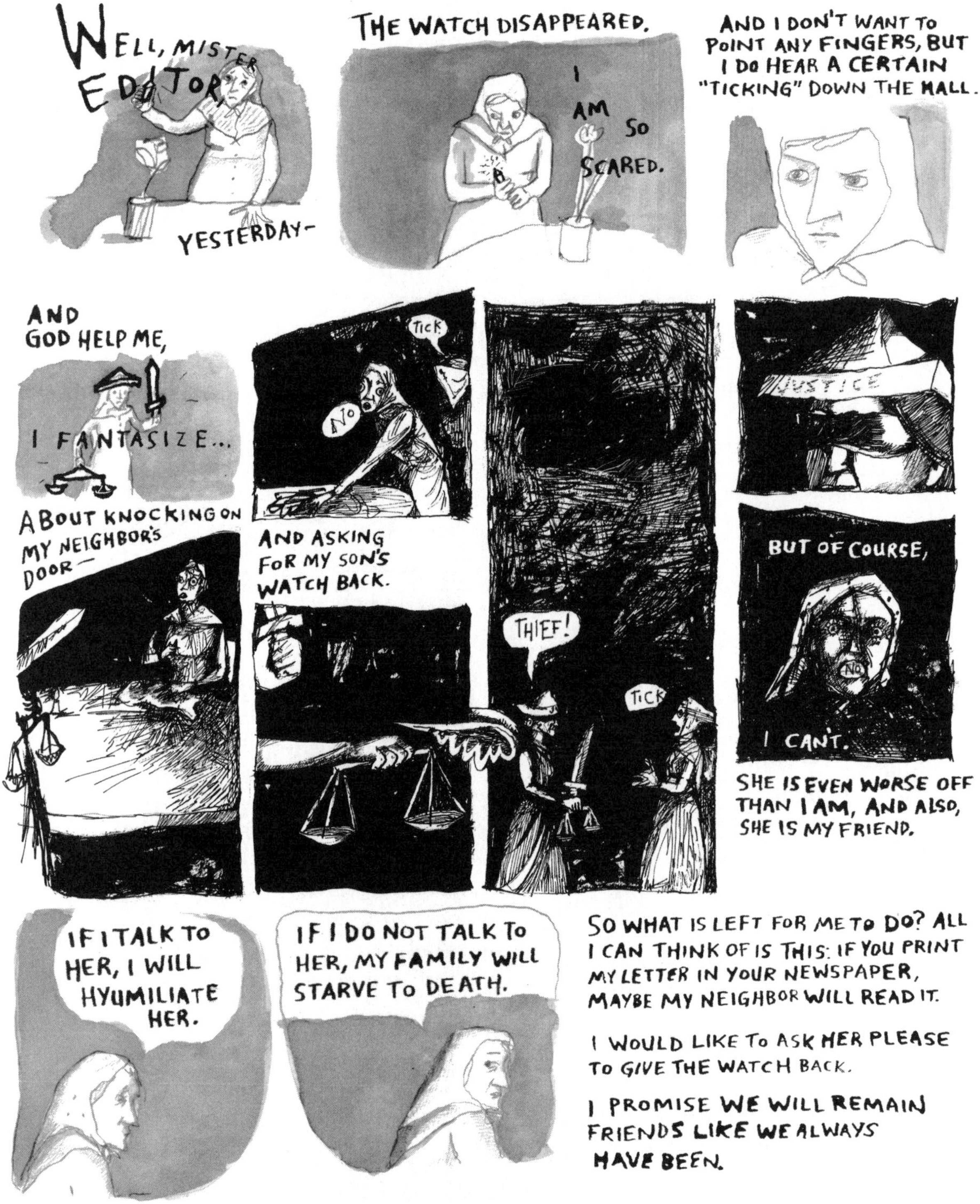
WELL, MISTER EDITOR,
YESTERDAY-
THE WATCH DISAPPEARED.
I AM SO SCARED.
AND I DON'T WANT TO POINT ANY FINGERS, BUT I DO HEAR A CERTAIN "TICKING" DOWN THE HALL.
AND GOD HELP ME,
I FANTASIZE...
TICK
NO
JUSTICE
ABOUT KNOCKING ON MY NEIGHBOR'S DOOR—
AND ASKING FOR MY SON'S WATCH BACK.
THIEF!
TICK
BUT OF COURSE,
NO
I CAN'T.
SHE IS EVEN WORSE OFF THAN I AM, AND ALSO, SHE IS MY FRIEND.
IF I TALK TO HER, I WILL HYUMILIATE HER.
IF I DO NOT TALK TO HER, MY FAMILY WILL STARVE TO DEATH.
SO WHAT IS LEFT FOR ME TO DO? ALL I CAN THINK OF IS THIS: IF YOU PRINT MY LETTER IN YOUR NEWSPAPER, MAYBE MY NEIGHBOR WILL READ IT.
I WOULD LIKE TO ASK HER PLEASE TO GIVE THE WATCH BACK.
I PROMISE WE WILL REMAIN FRIENDS LIKE WE ALWAYS HAVE BEEN.

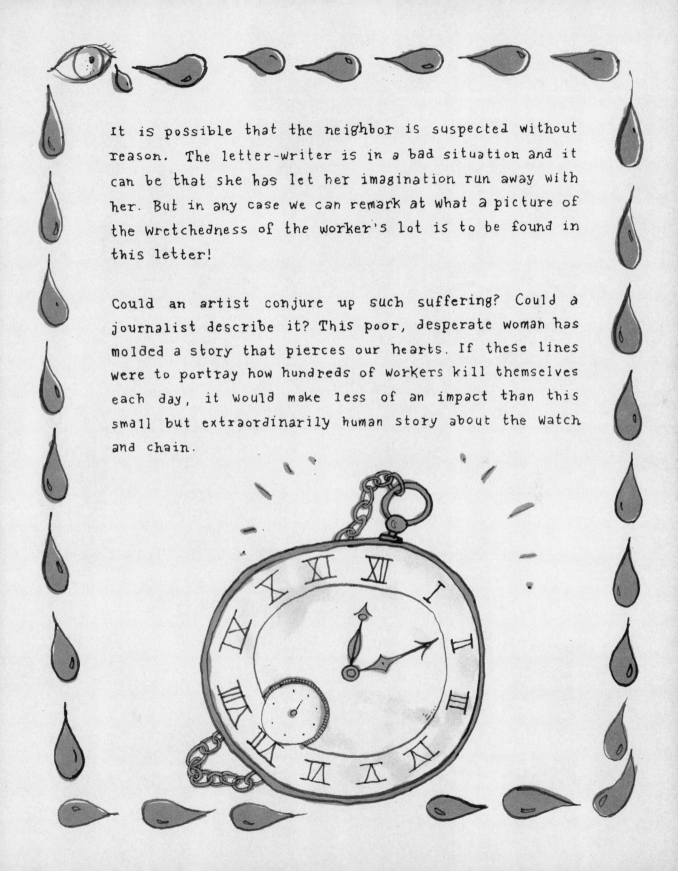

It is possible that the neighbor is suspected without reason. The letter-writer is in a bad situation and it can be that she has let her imagination run away with her. But in any case we can remark at what a picture of the wretchedness of the worker's lot is to be found in this letter!

Could an artist conjure up such suffering? Could a journalist describe it? This poor, desperate woman has molded a story that pierces our hearts. If these lines were to portray how hundreds of workers kill themselves each day, it would make less of an impact than this small but extraordinarily human story about the watch and chain.

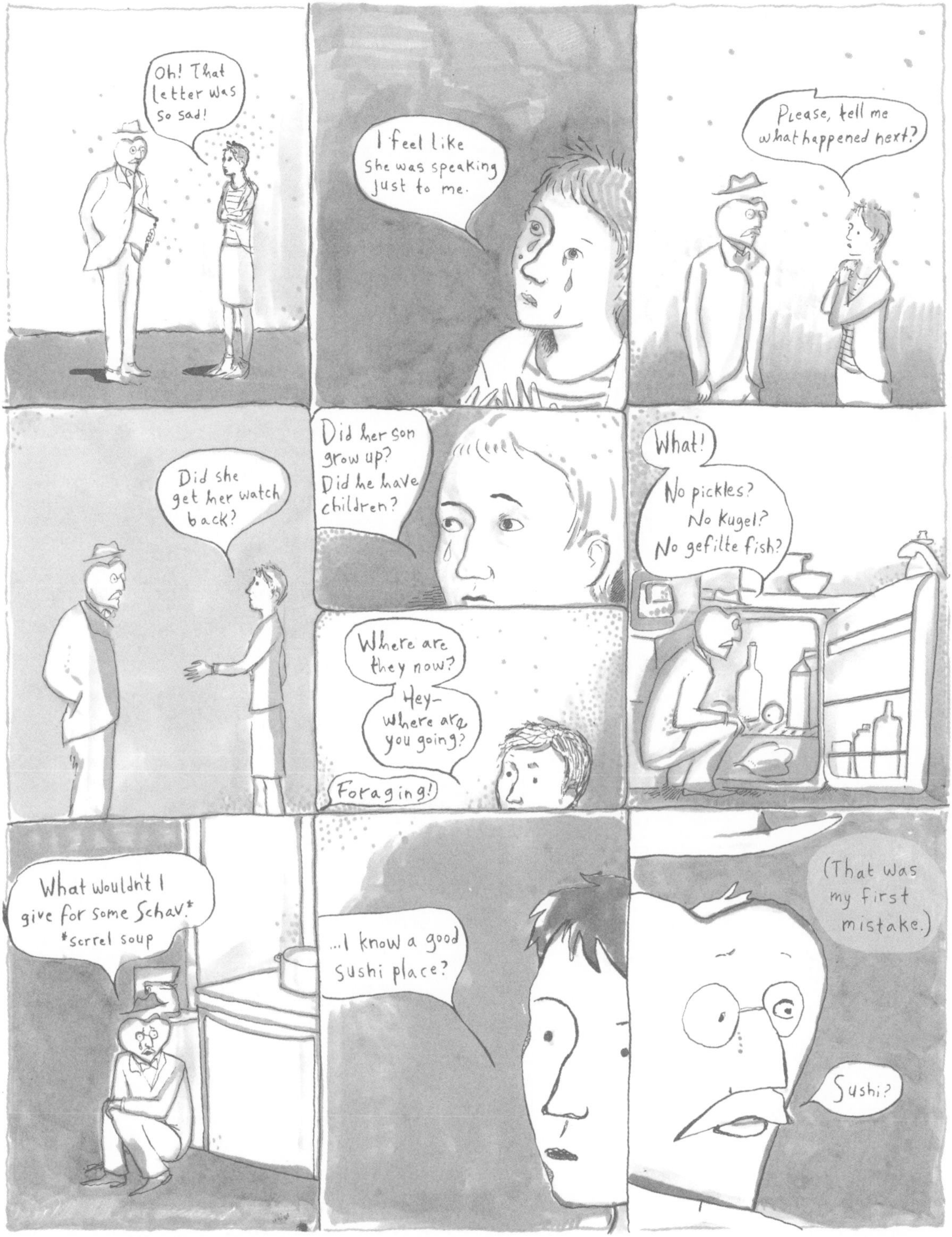
Oh! That letter was so sad!
I feel like she was speaking just to me.
Please, tell me what happened next?
Did she get her watch back?
Did her son grow up? Did he have children?
Where are they now?
Hey- Where are you going?
Foraging!
What!
No pickles? No kugel? No gefilte fish?
What wouldn't I give for some Schav!*
*sorrel soup
...I know a good sushi place?
(That was my first mistake.)
Sushi?

2

FATHER?

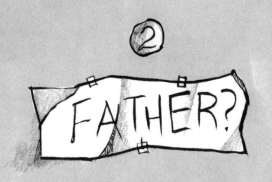

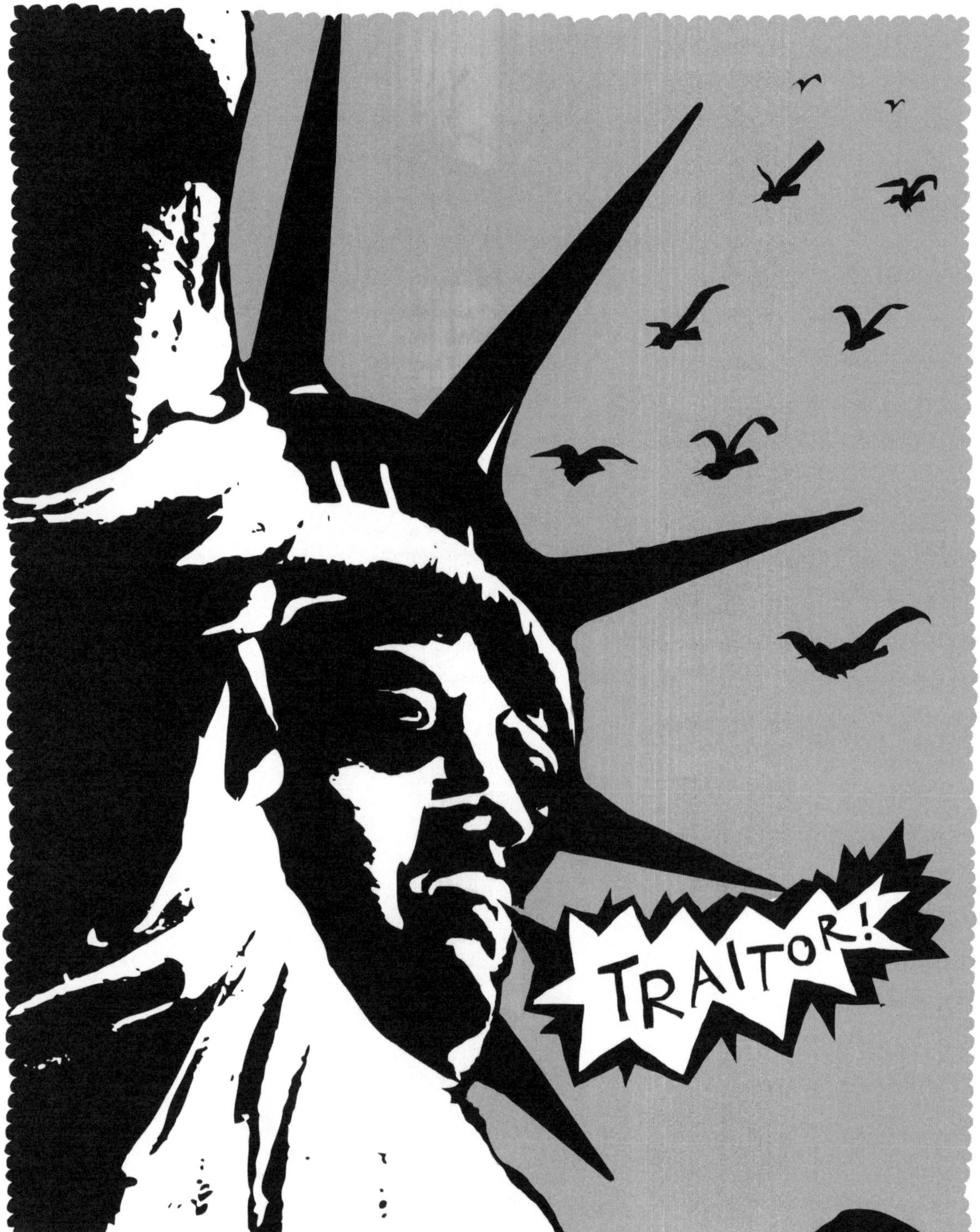
TRAITOR!

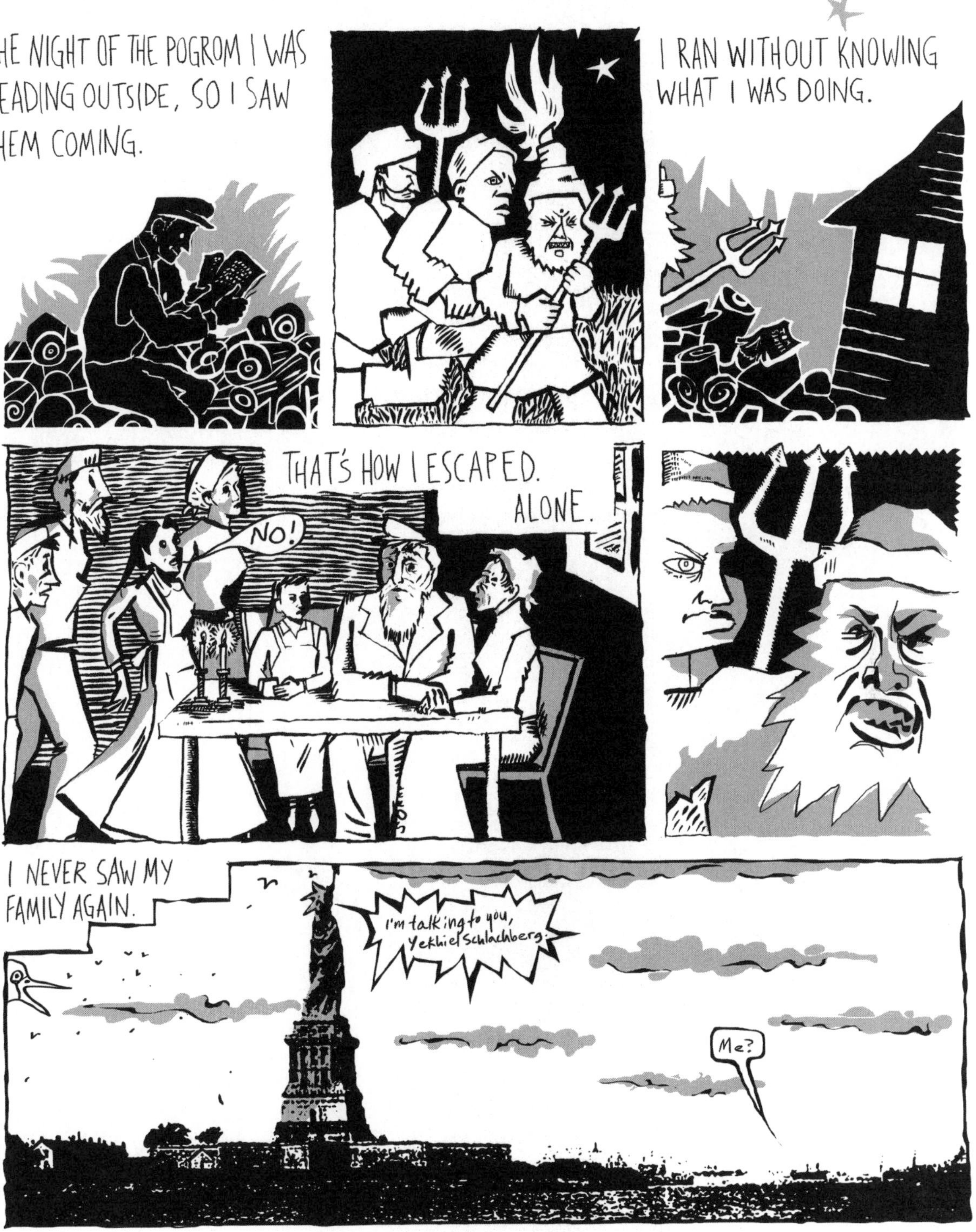
THE NIGHT OF THE POGROM I WAS READING OUTSIDE, SO I SAW THEM COMING.
I RAN WITHOUT KNOWING WHAT I WAS DOING.
THAT'S HOW I ESCAPED.
ALONE.
NO!
I NEVER SAW MY FAMILY AGAIN.
I'm talking to you, Yekhiel Schlachberg.
Me?

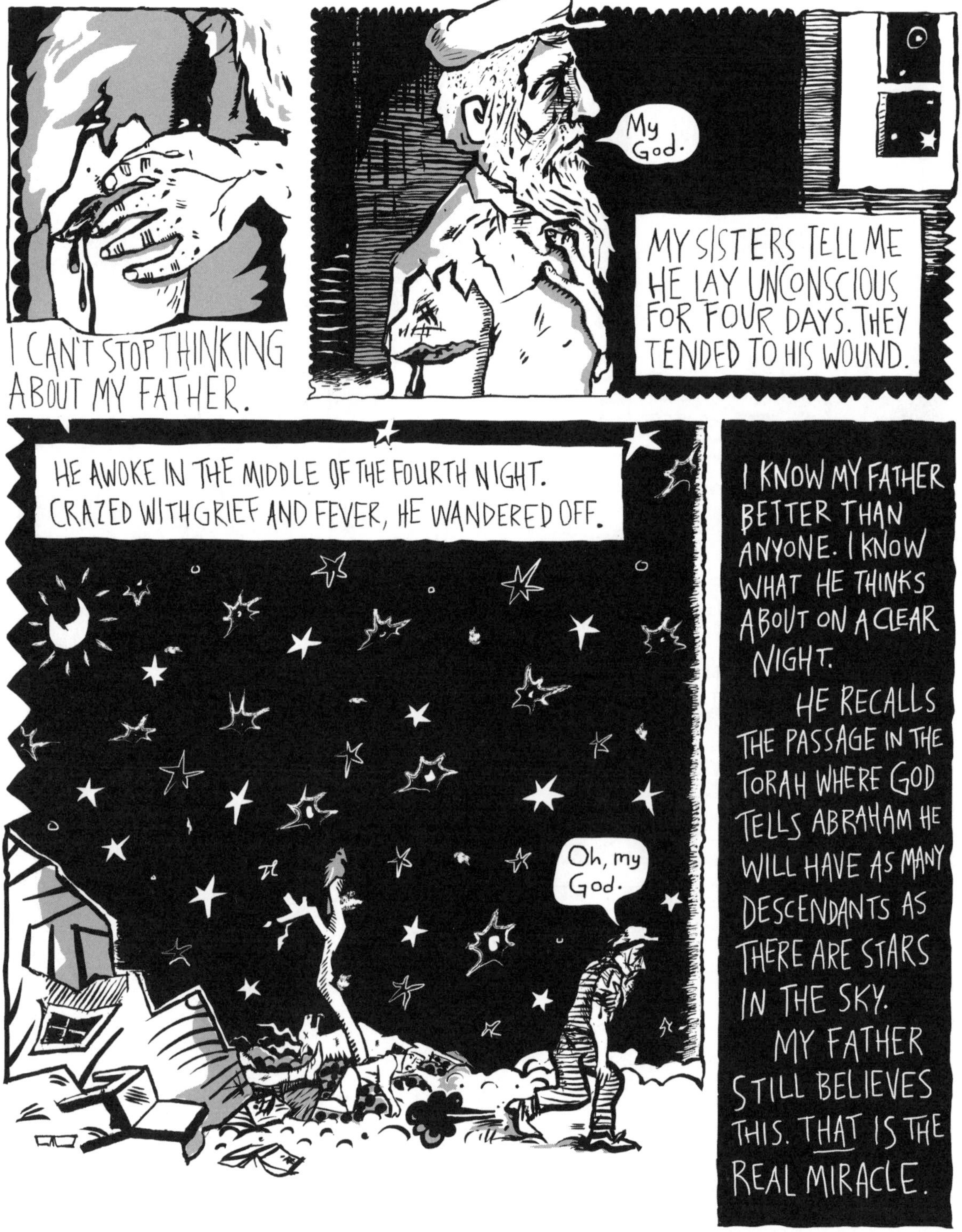
I CAN'T STOP THINKING ABOUT MY FATHER.
My God.
MY SISTERS TELL ME HE LAY UNCONSCIOUS FOR FOUR DAYS. THEY TENDED TO HIS WOUND.
HE AWOKE IN THE MIDDLE OF THE FOURTH NIGHT. CRAZED WITH GRIEF AND FEVER, HE WANDERED OFF.
Oh, my God.
I KNOW MY FATHER BETTER THAN ANYONE. I KNOW WHAT HE THINKS ABOUT ON A CLEAR NIGHT.
HE RECALLS THE PASSAGE IN THE TORAH WHERE GOD TELLS ABRAHAM HE WILL HAVE AS MANY DESCENDANTS AS THERE ARE STARS IN THE SKY.
MY FATHER STILL BELIEVES THIS. THAT IS THE REAL MIRACLE.

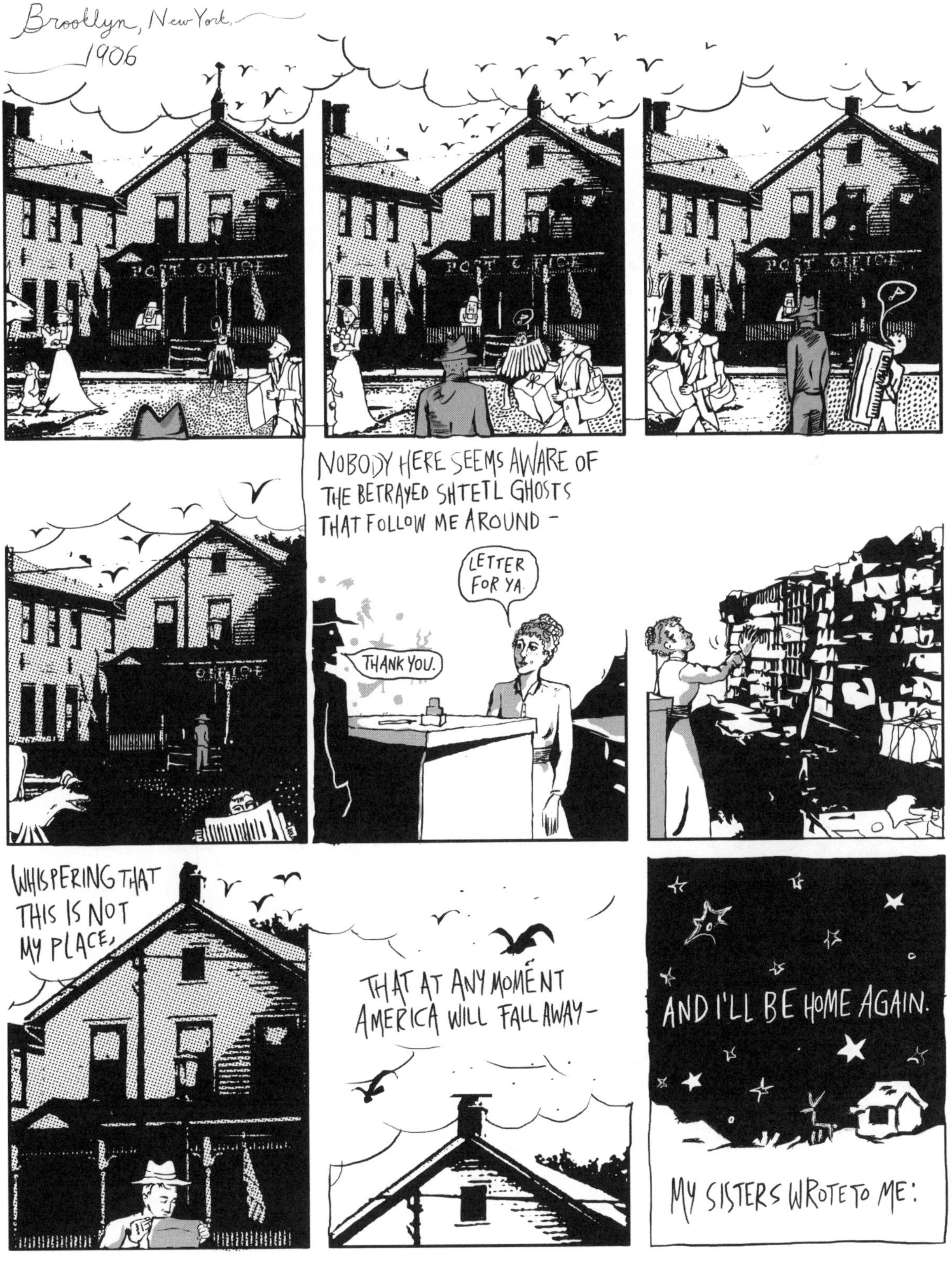
Brooklyn, New York, 1906
POST OFFICE
NOBODY HERE SEEMS AWARE OF THE BETRAYED SHTETL GHOSTS THAT FOLLOW ME AROUND -
LETTER FOR YA.
THANK YOU.
WHISPERING THAT THIS IS NOT MY PLACE,
THAT AT ANY MOMENT AMERICA WILL FALL AWAY-
AND I'LL BE HOME AGAIN.
MY SISTERS WROTE TO ME:

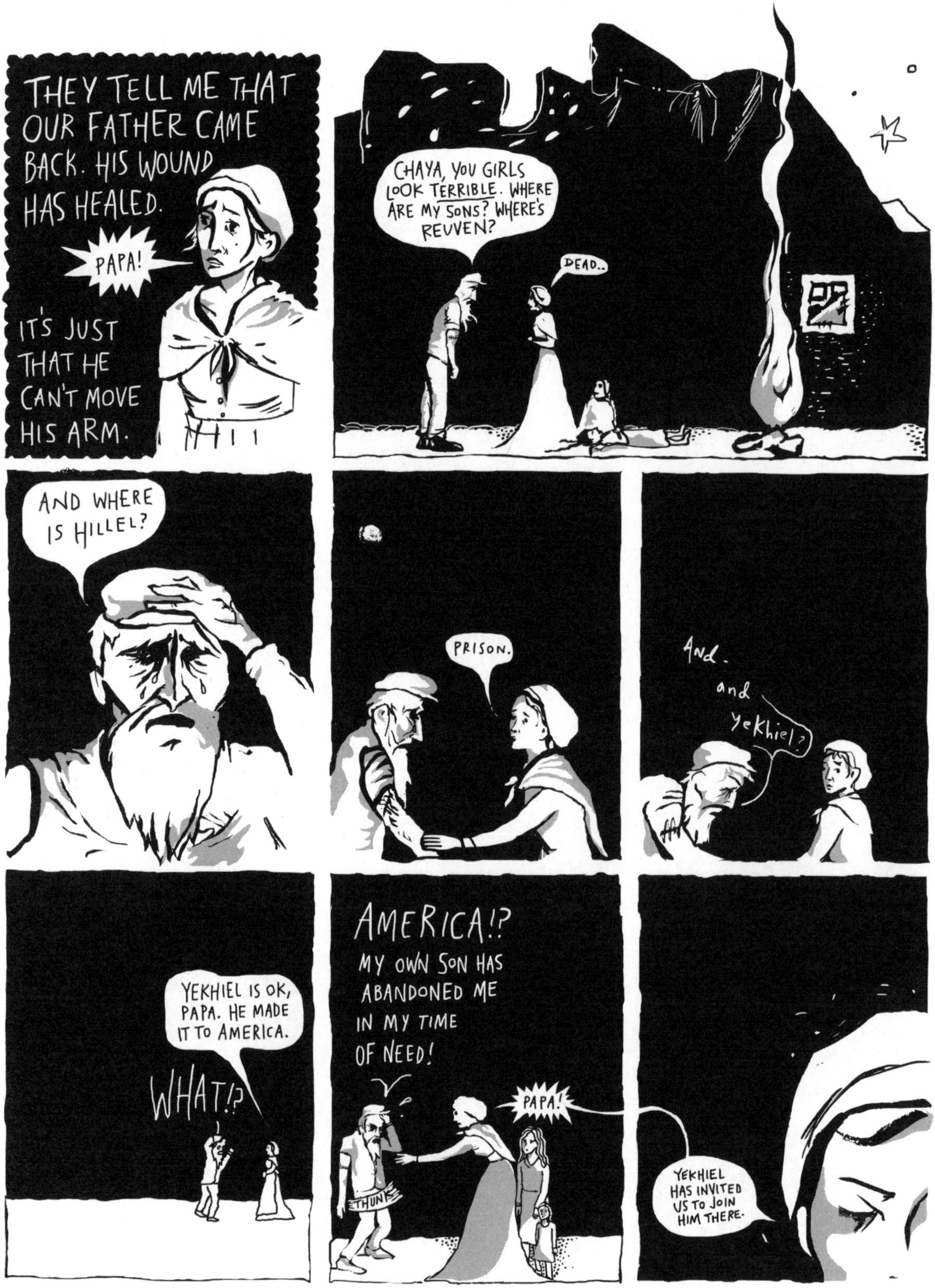
THEY TELL ME THAT OUR FATHER CAME BACK. HIS WOUND HAS HEALED.
PAPA!
IT'S JUST THAT HE CAN'T MOVE HIS ARM.
CHAYA, YOU GIRLS LOOK TERRIBLE. WHERE ARE MY SONS? WHERE'S REUVEN?
DEAD..
AND WHERE IS HILLEL?
PRISON.
And.
and
yekhiel?
YEKHIEL IS OK, PAPA. HE MADE IT TO AMERICA.
WHAT!?
AMERICA!? MY OWN SON HAS ABANDONED ME IN MY TIME OF NEED!
THUNK
PAPA!
YEKHIEL HAS INVITED US TO JOIN HIM THERE.

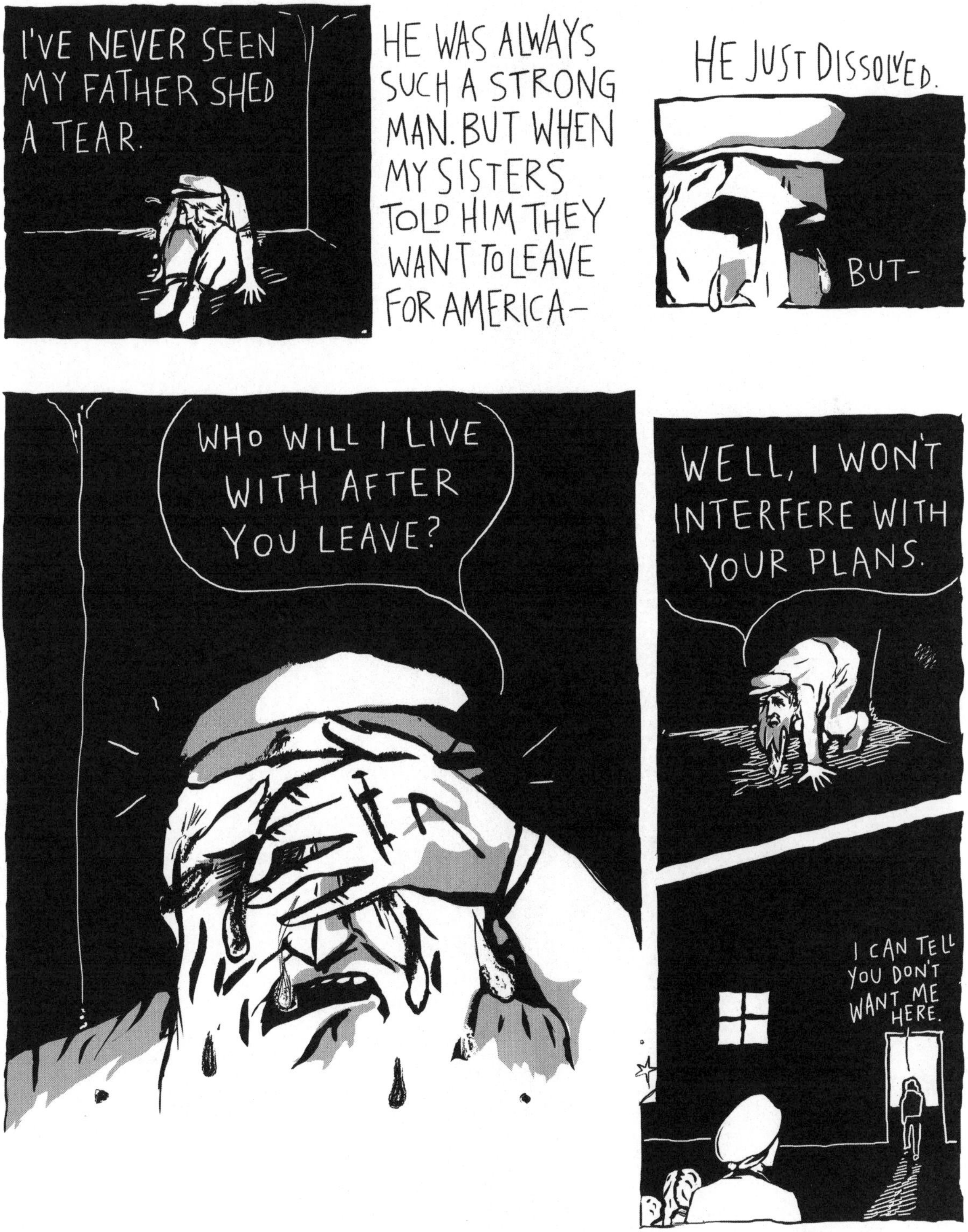
I'VE NEVER SEEN MY FATHER SHED A TEAR.
HE WAS ALWAYS SUCH A STRONG MAN. BUT WHEN MY SISTERS TOLD HIM THEY WANT TO LEAVE FOR AMERICA-
HE JUST DISSOLVED.
BUT-
WHO WILL I LIVE WITH AFTER YOU LEAVE?
WELL, I WON'T INTERFERE WITH YOUR PLANS.
I CAN TELL YOU DON'T WANT ME HERE.

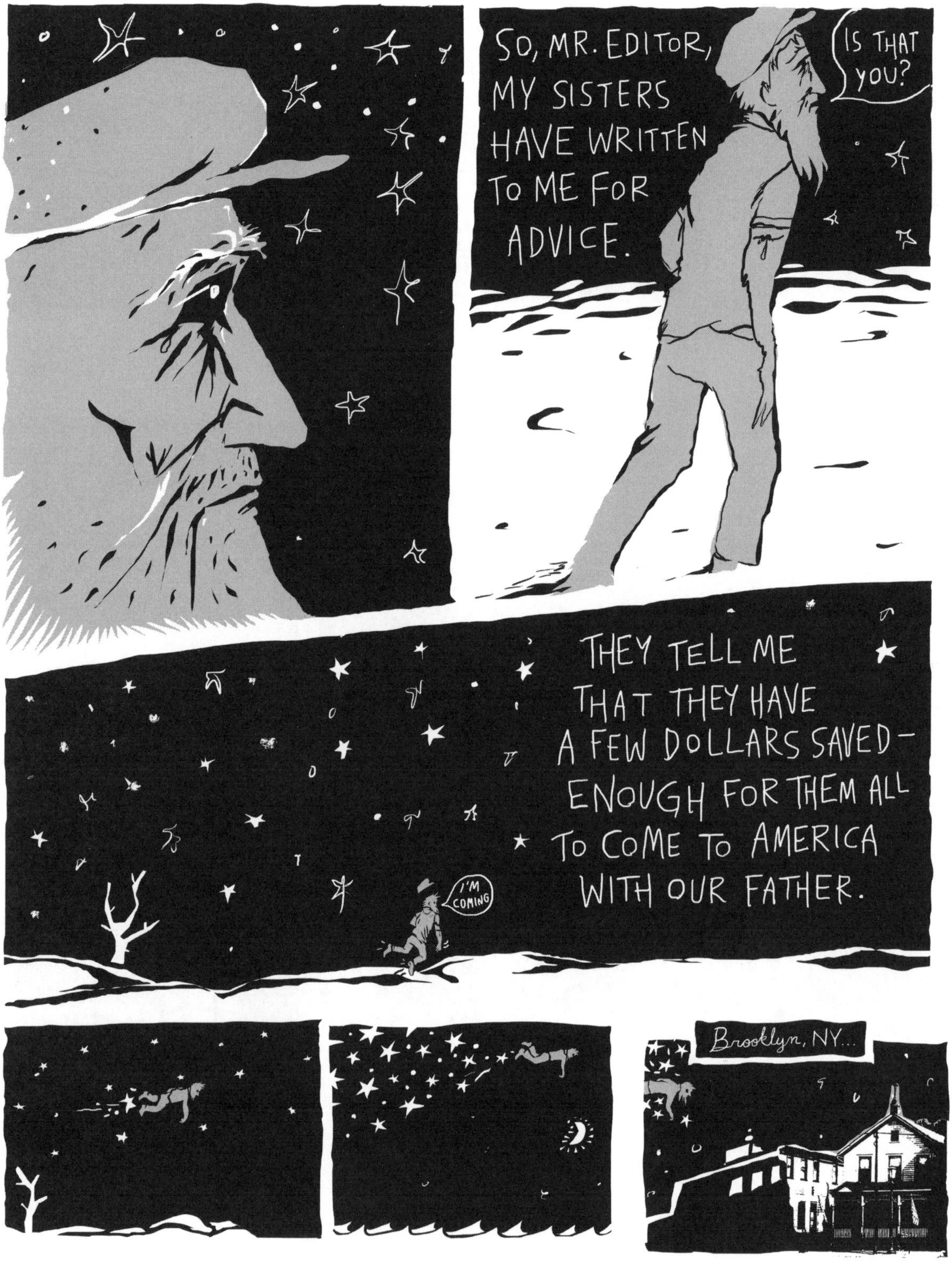
SO, MR. EDITOR, MY SISTERS HAVE WRITTEN TO ME FOR ADVICE.
IS THAT YOU?
THEY TELL ME THAT THEY HAVE A FEW DOLLARS SAVED— ENOUGH FOR THEM ALL TO COME TO AMERICA WITH OUR FATHER.
I'M COMING
Brooklyn, NY...

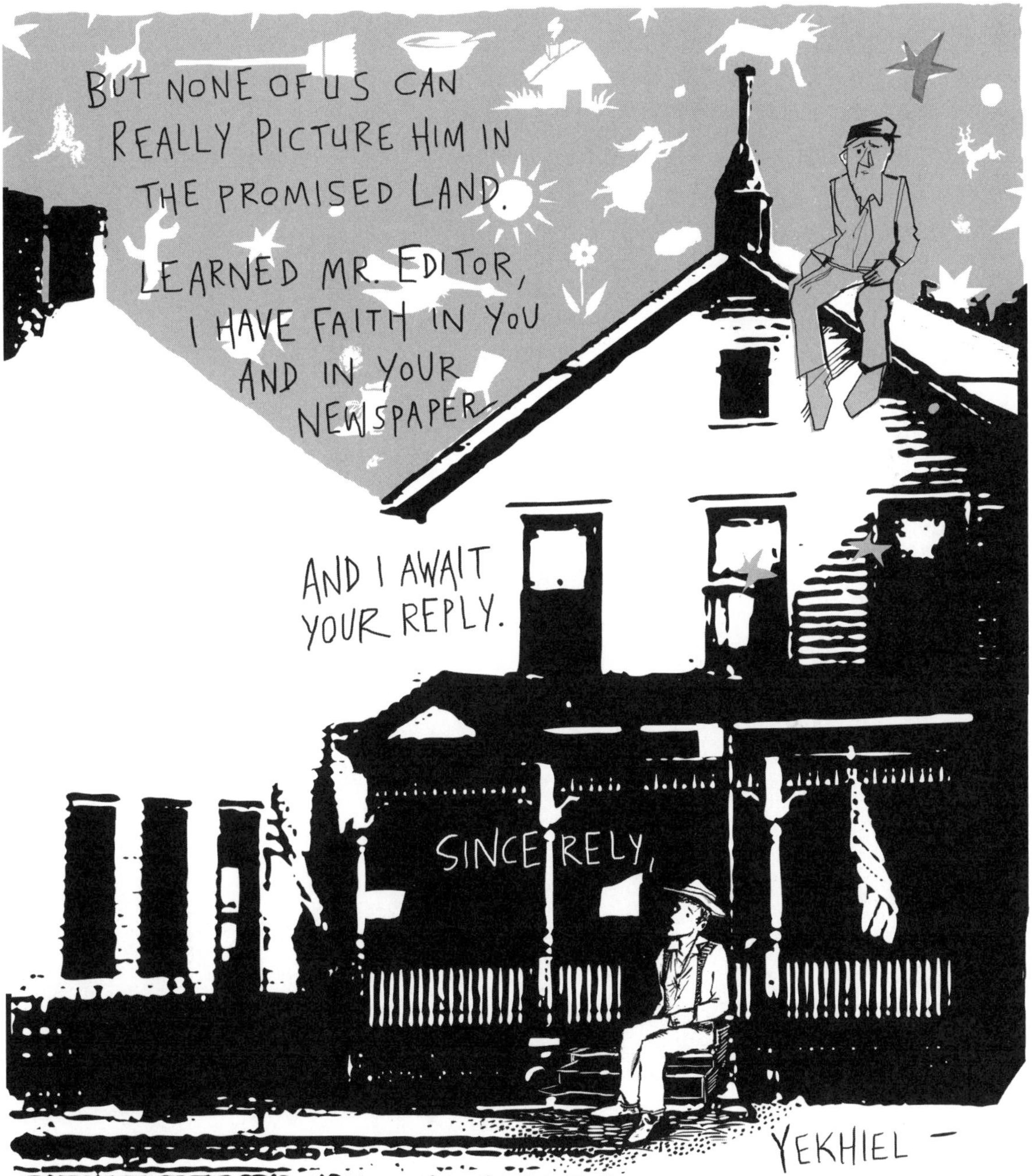
BUT NONE OF US CAN REALLY PICTURE HIM IN THE PROMISED LAND.
LEARNED MR. EDITOR, I HAVE FAITH IN YOU AND IN YOUR NEWSPAPER.
AND I AWAIT YOUR REPLY.
SINCERELY,
YEKHIEL SCHLACHBERG

Brooklyn, New York

For various reasons we need to answer this heart-
wrenching letter privately. The writer should send us
his full address.

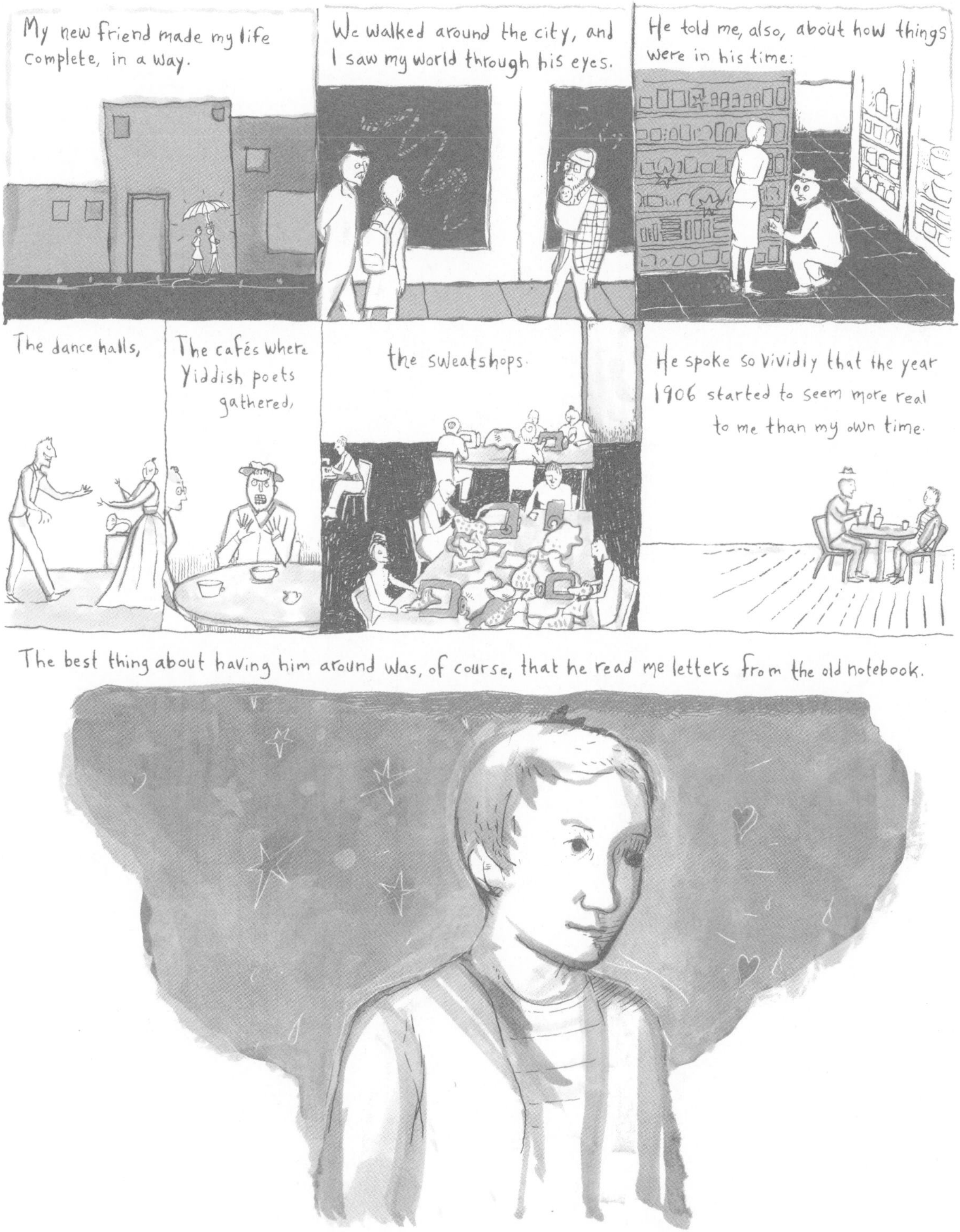
My new friend made my life complete, in a way.
We walked around the city, and I saw my world through his eyes.
He told me, also, about how things were in his time:
The dance halls,
The cafés where Yiddish poets gathered,
the sweatshops.
He spoke so vividly that the year 1906 started to seem more real to me than my own time.
The best thing about having him around was, of course, that he read me letters from the old notebook.

3

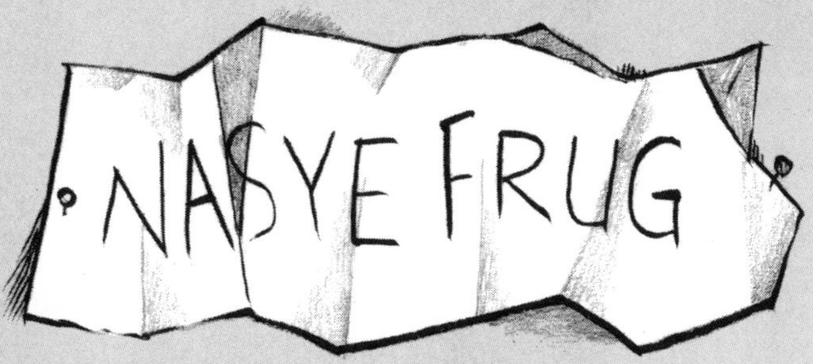
NASYE FRUG

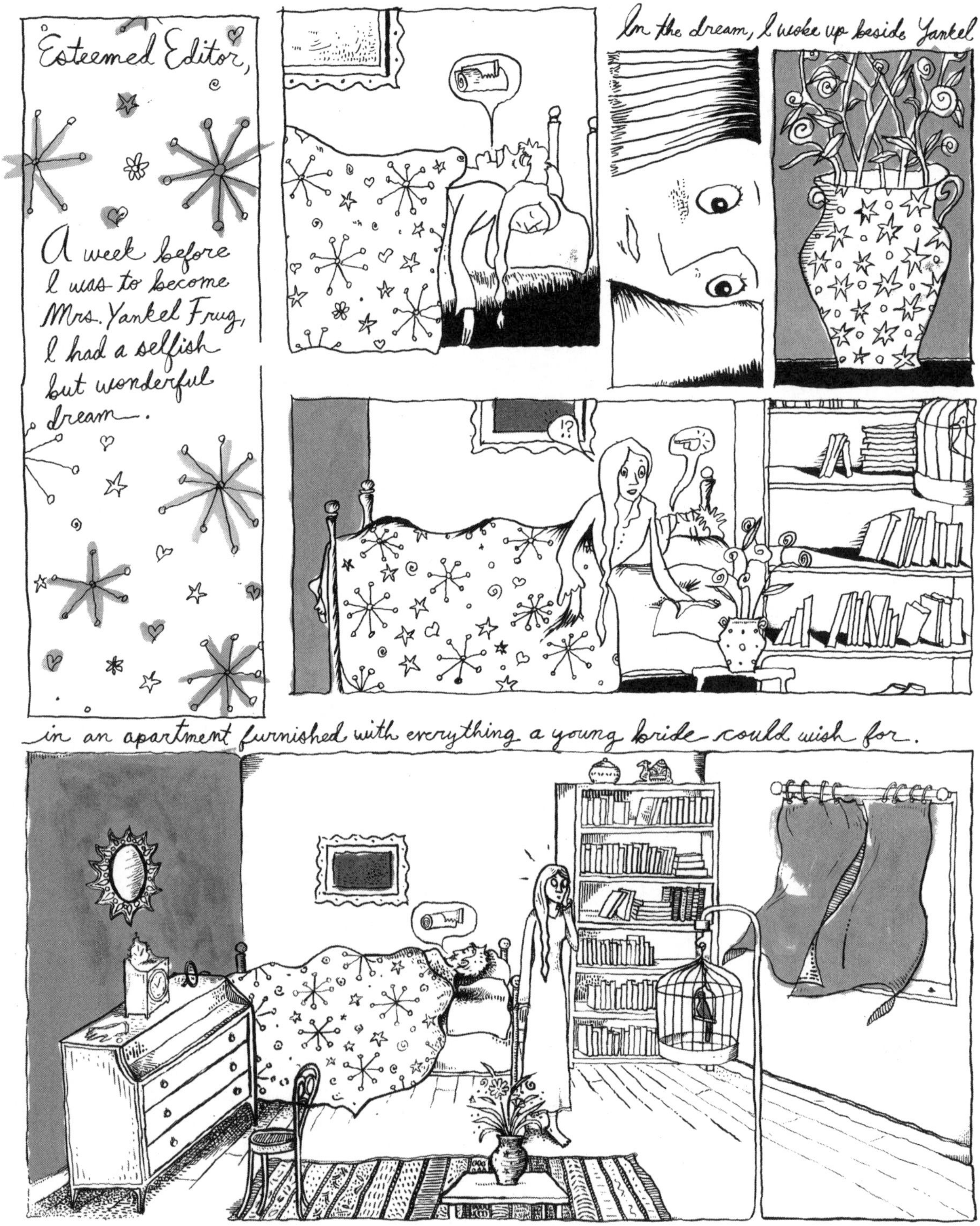
Esteemed Editor,
A week before I was to become Mrs. Yankel Frug, I had a selfish but wonderful dream.
In the dream, I woke up beside Yankel
!?
in an apartment furnished with everything a young bride could wish for.

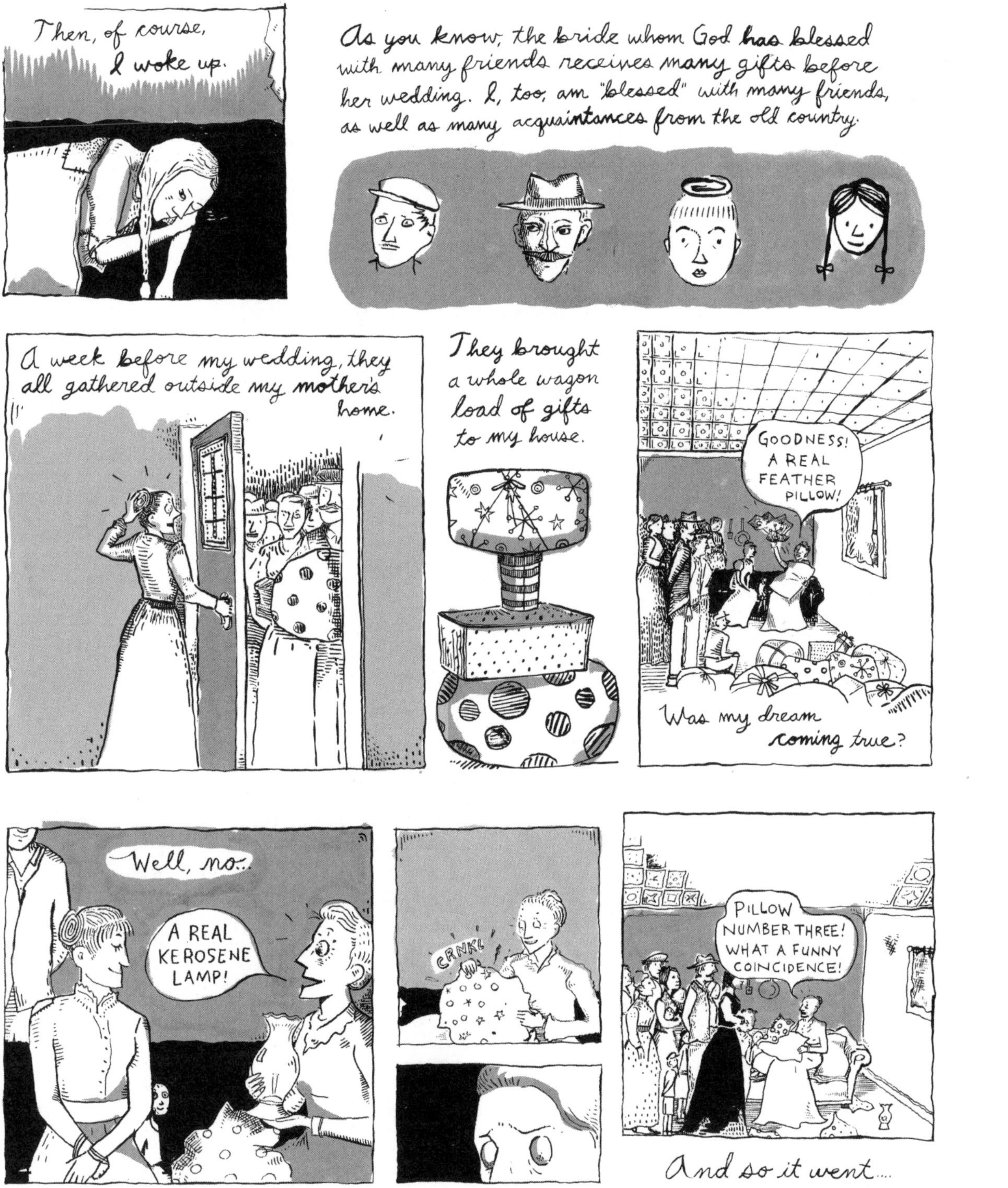
Then, of course, I woke up.
As you know, the bride whom God has blessed with many friends receives many gifts before her wedding. I, too, am "blessed" with many friends, as well as many acquaintances from the old country.
A week before my wedding, they all gathered outside my mother's home.
They brought a whole wagon load of gifts to my house.
GOODNESS! A REAL FEATHER PILLOW!
Was my dream coming true?
Well, no...
A REAL KEROSENE LAMP!
CRNKL
PILLOW NUMBER THREE! WHAT A FUNNY COINCIDENCE!
And so it went....

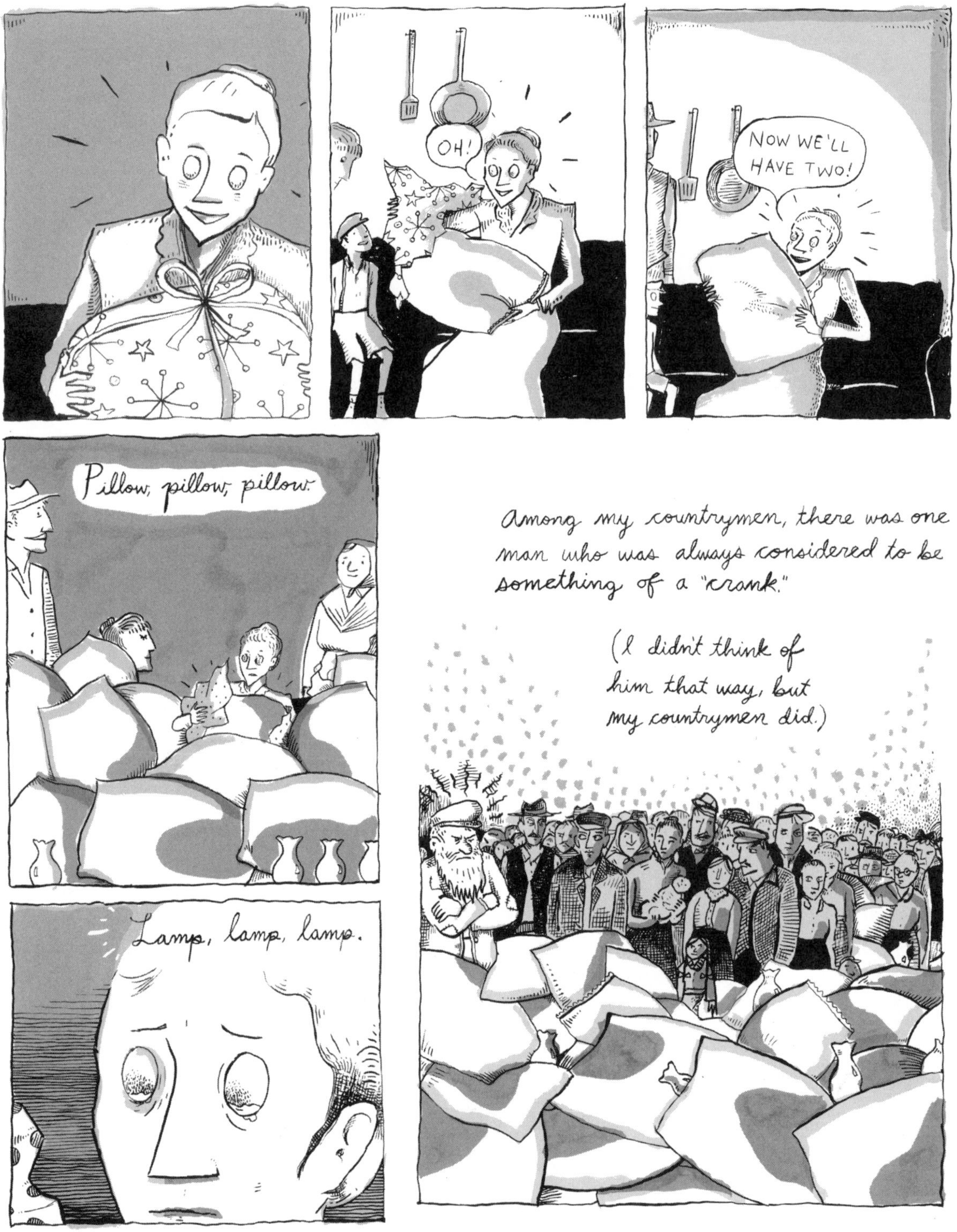
OH!
NOW WE'LL HAVE TWO!
Pillow, pillow, pillow.
Lamp, lamp, lamp.
Among my countrymen, there was one man who was always considered to be something of a "crank."
(I didn't think of him that way, but my countrymen did.)

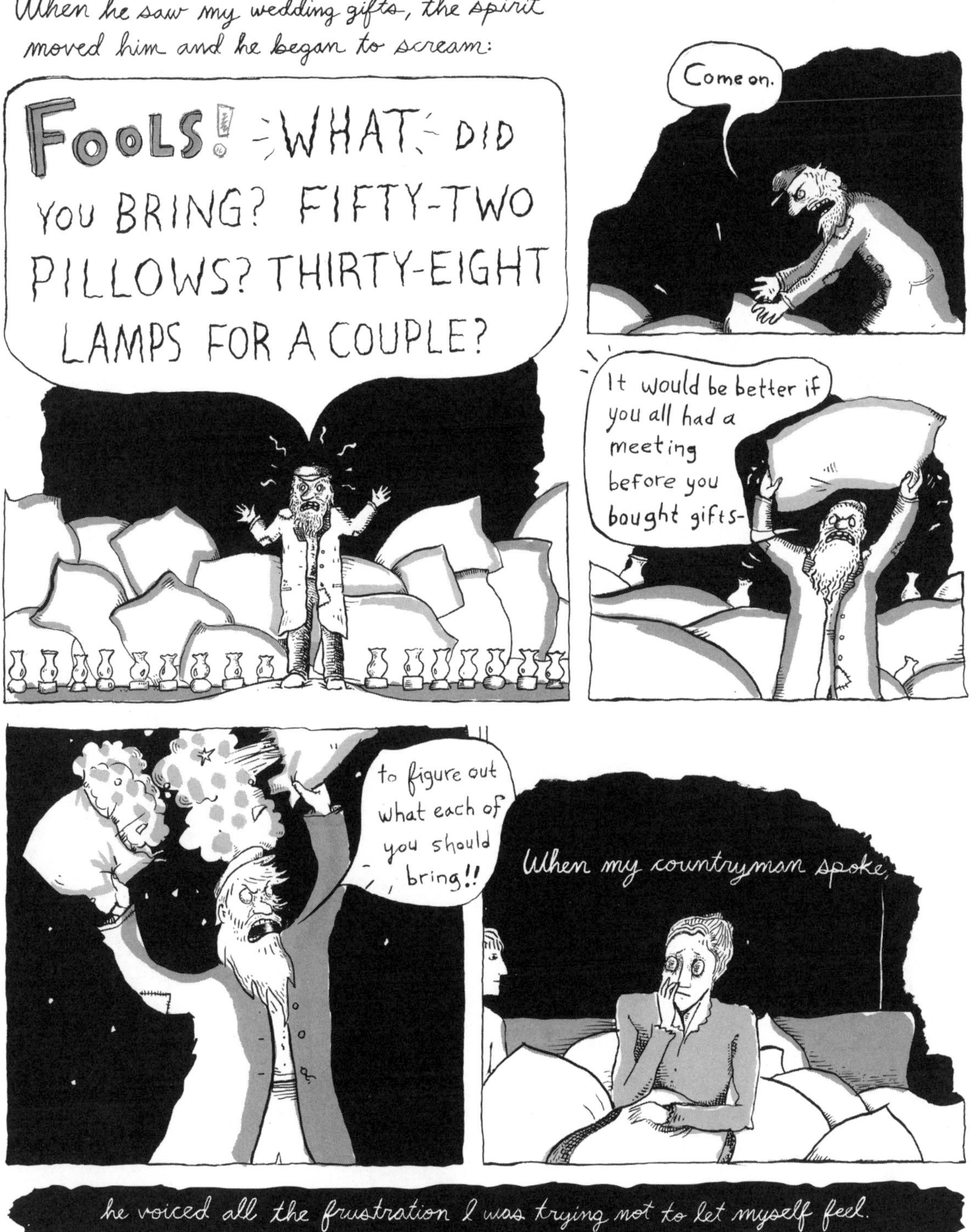
When he saw my wedding gifts, the spirit moved him and he began to scream:
FOOLS! WHAT DID YOU BRING? FIFTY-TWO PILLOWS? THIRTY-EIGHT LAMPS FOR A COUPLE?
Come on.
It would be better if you all had a meeting before you bought gifts-
to figure out what each of you should bring!!
When my countryman spoke,
he voiced all the frustration I was trying not to let myself feel.

Yankel and I were married several days ago.
We are very happy together, but something still bothers me.
DEAR... MISSES... BIRNBAUM... THANK... YOU... FOR... THE... BEAUTIFUL... PILLOW...
Esteemed Mr. Editor,
YANKEL, WHAT ARE YOU WRITING?
EIGHTY-ONE THANK-YOU NOTES.
GET SOME SLEEP.
Am I a bad person for feeling so ungrateful? Or did the "crank" have a point?

Your countryman is no "fool," not by any measure. We know plenty of cases in which relatives and acquaintances bring the bride and groom gifts and when the couple "wakes up" from the dream that they already have a fully furnished house, it turns out that they've ended up with a kitchen with ten chopping knives, five boards for soaking meat, a few dozen little goblets and so forth. Your "fool's" plan to agree upon what you and your groom need in advance is a very good plan indeed. Your "dream" of having a decent life in America would be better classified as a "reasonable expectation."

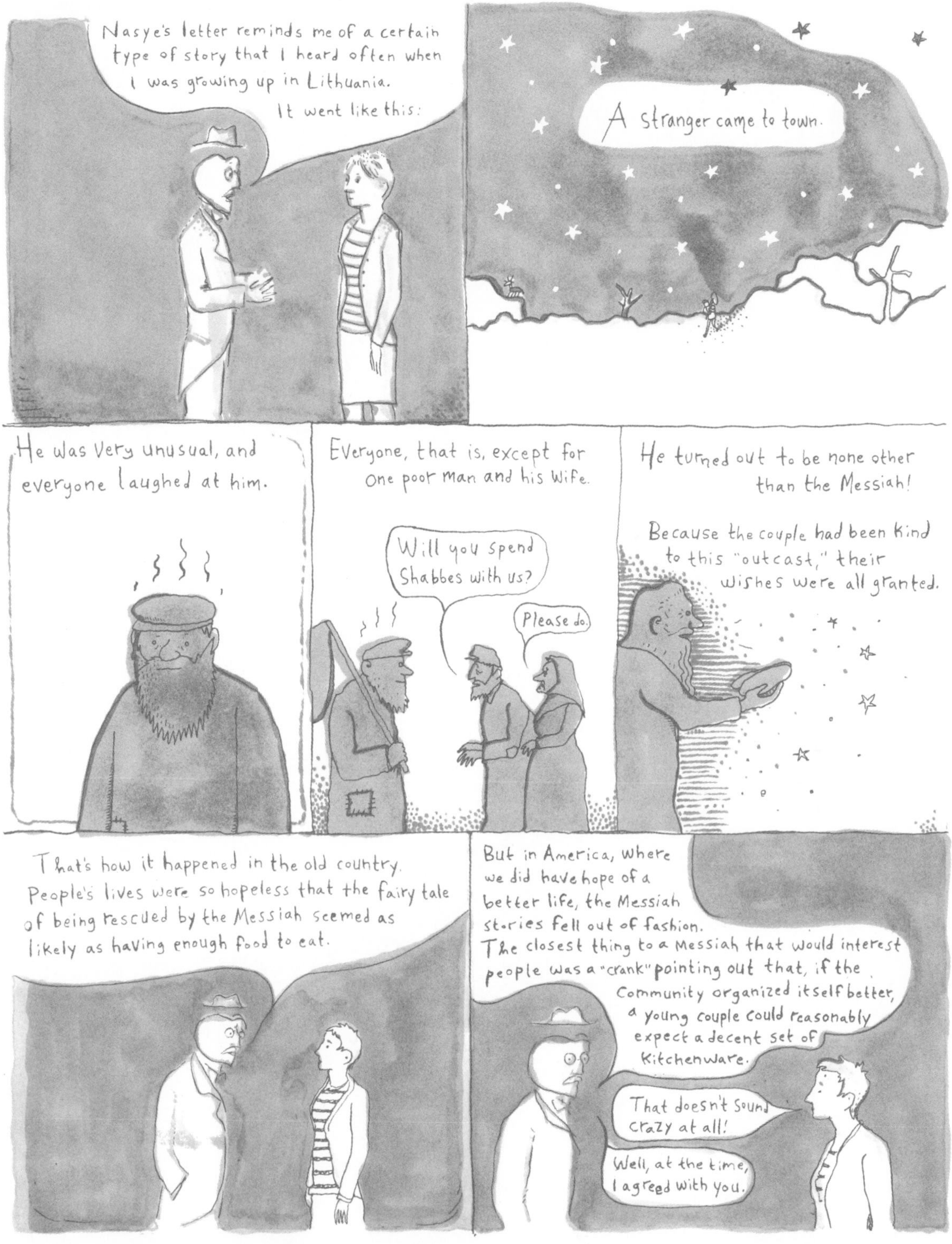
Nasye's letter reminds me of a certain type of story that I heard often when I was growing up in Lithuania.
It went like this:
A stranger came to town.
He was very unusual, and everyone laughed at him.
Everyone, that is, except for one poor man and his wife.
Will you spend Shabbes with us?
Please do.
He turned out to be none other than the Messiah!
Because the couple had been kind to this "outcast," their wishes were all granted.
That's how it happened in the old country. People's lives were so hopeless that the fairy tale of being rescued by the Messiah seemed as likely as having enough food to eat.
But in America, where we did have hope of a better life, the Messiah stories fell out of fashion.
The closest thing to a Messiah that would interest people was a "crank" pointing out that, if the community organized itself better, a young couple could reasonably expect a decent set of kitchenware.
That doesn't sound crazy at all!
Well, at the time, I agreed with you.

4

A MAD(?) BARBER

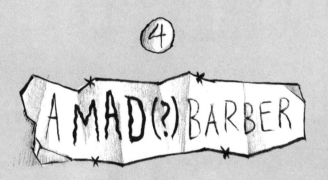

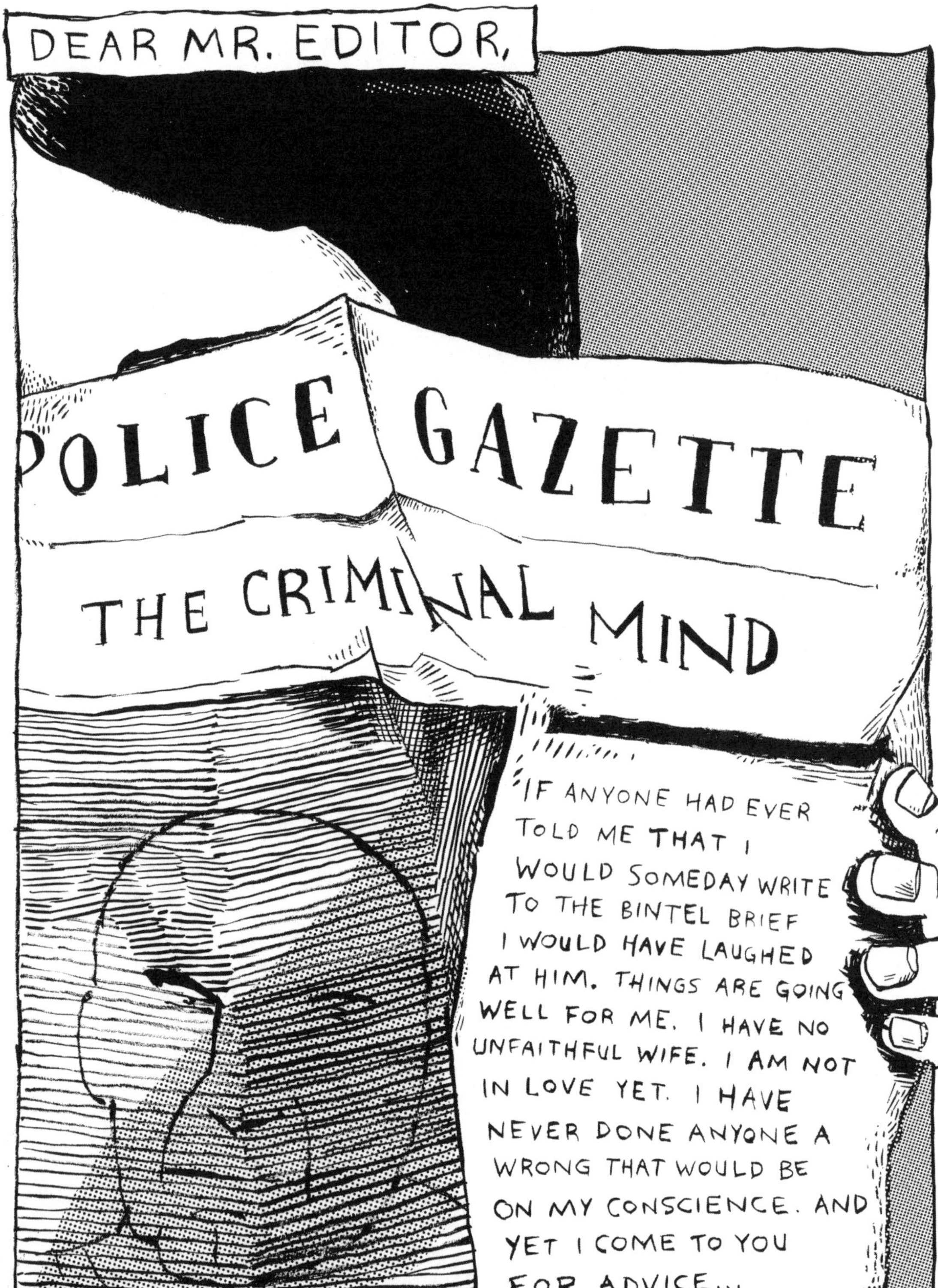
DEAR MR. EDITOR,
POLICE GAZETTE
THE CRIMINAL MIND
IF ANYONE HAD EVER TOLD ME THAT I WOULD SOMEDAY WRITE TO THE BINTEL BRIEF I WOULD HAVE LAUGHED AT HIM. THINGS ARE GOING WELL FOR ME. I HAVE NO UNFAITHFUL WIFE. I AM NOT IN LOVE YET. I HAVE NEVER DONE ANYONE A WRONG THAT WOULD BE ON MY CONSCIENCE. AND YET I COME TO YOU FOR ADVICE...

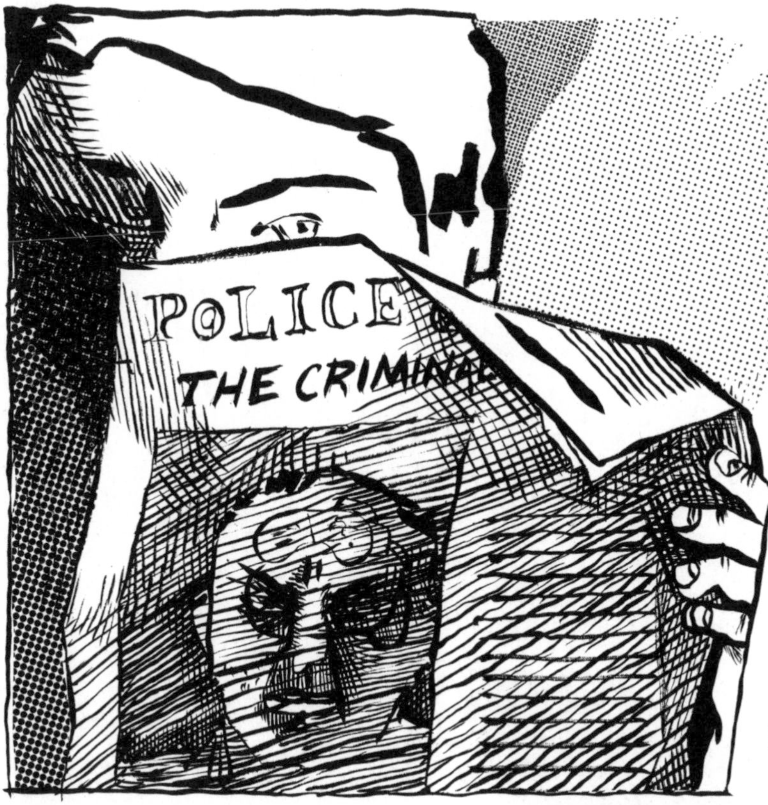
POLICE
THE CRIMIN

I AM A BARBER AND HAVE BEEN PRACTICING THE "ART" FOR TEN YEARS AND BECAME QUITE ADEPT AT IT. SOUNDS GOOD, YES? BUT THE FOLLOWING HAPPENED:

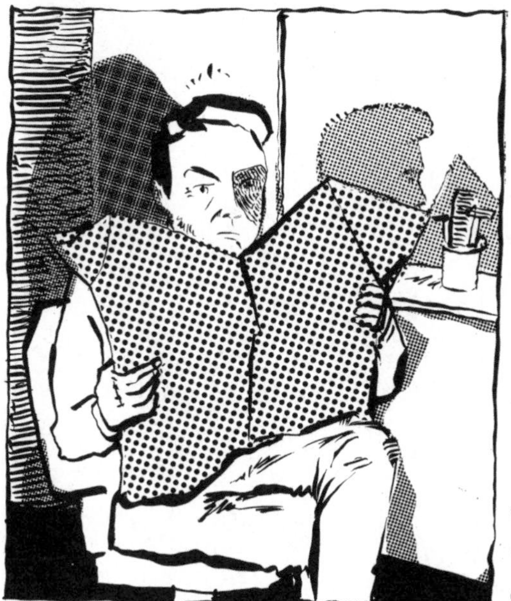

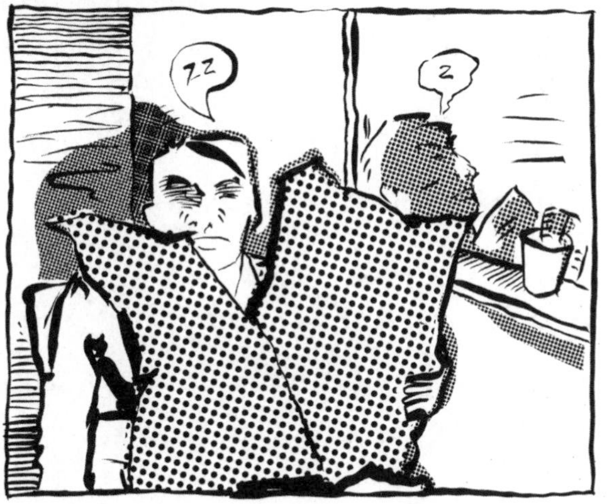
ZZ
Z

A FEW WEEKS AGO, ON A QUIET AFTERNOON WHEN THERE WERE NO CUSTOMERS AND THE BOSS WAS OUT SOMEWHERE, I DOZED OFF WHILE READING THE **POLICE GAZETTE**.

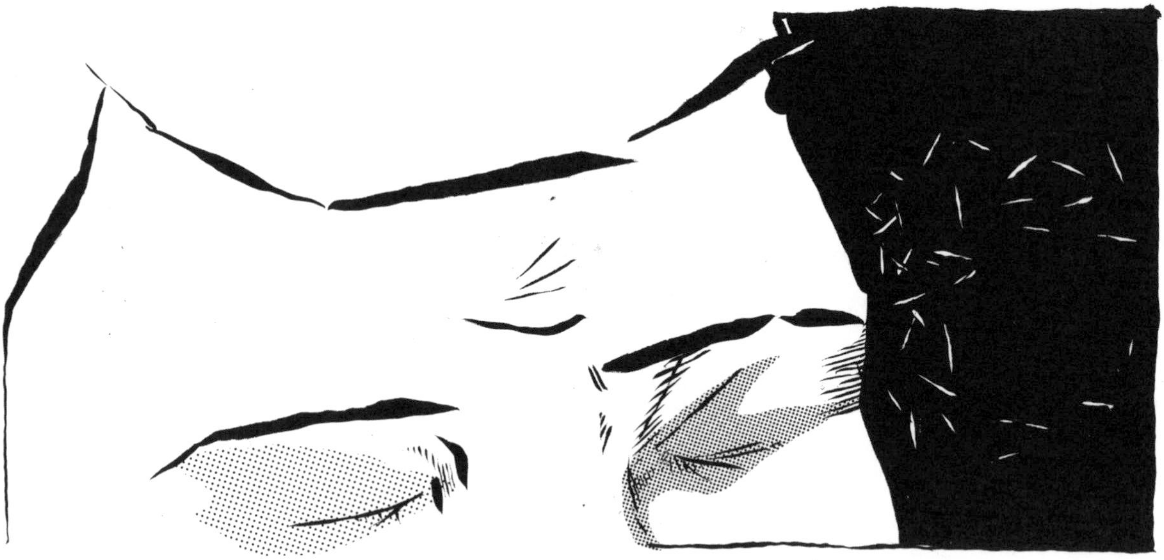

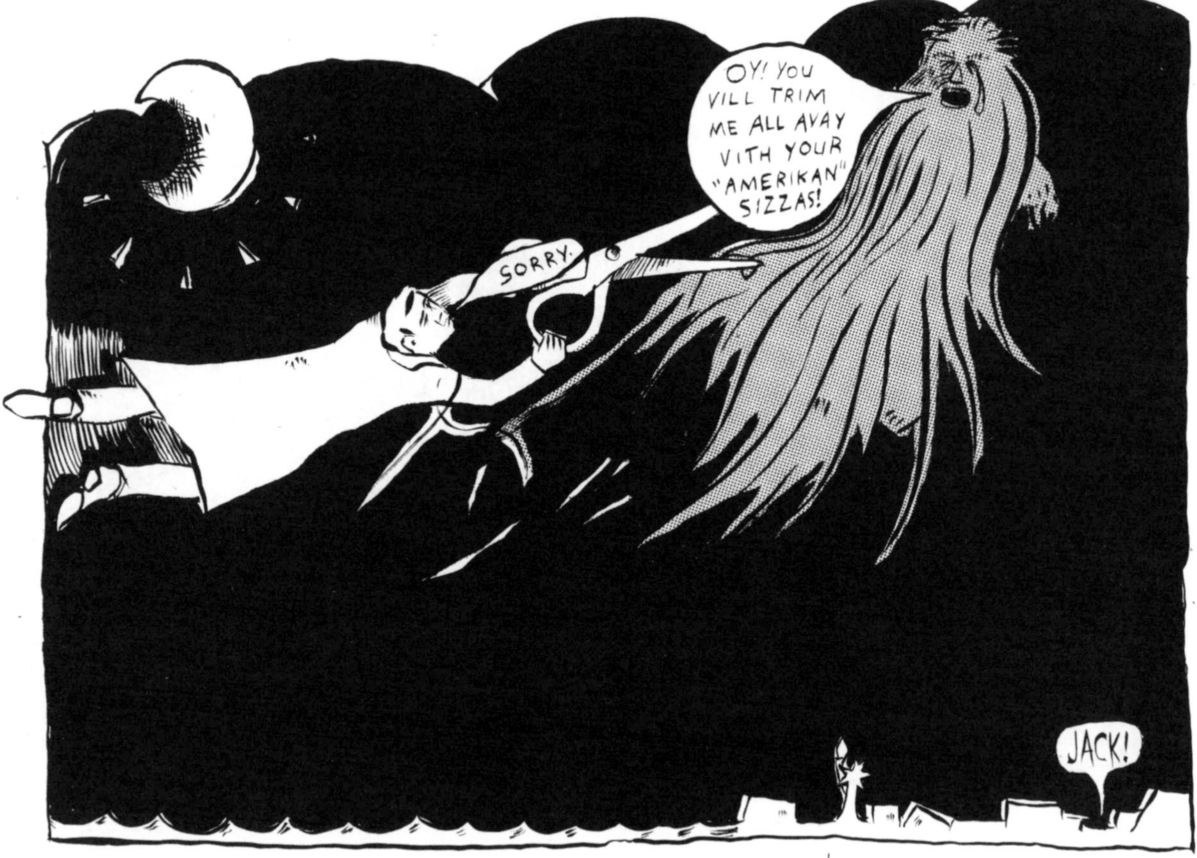
OY! YOU VILL TRIM ME ALL AVAY VITH YOUR "AMERIKAN" SIZZAS!
SORRY.
JACK!

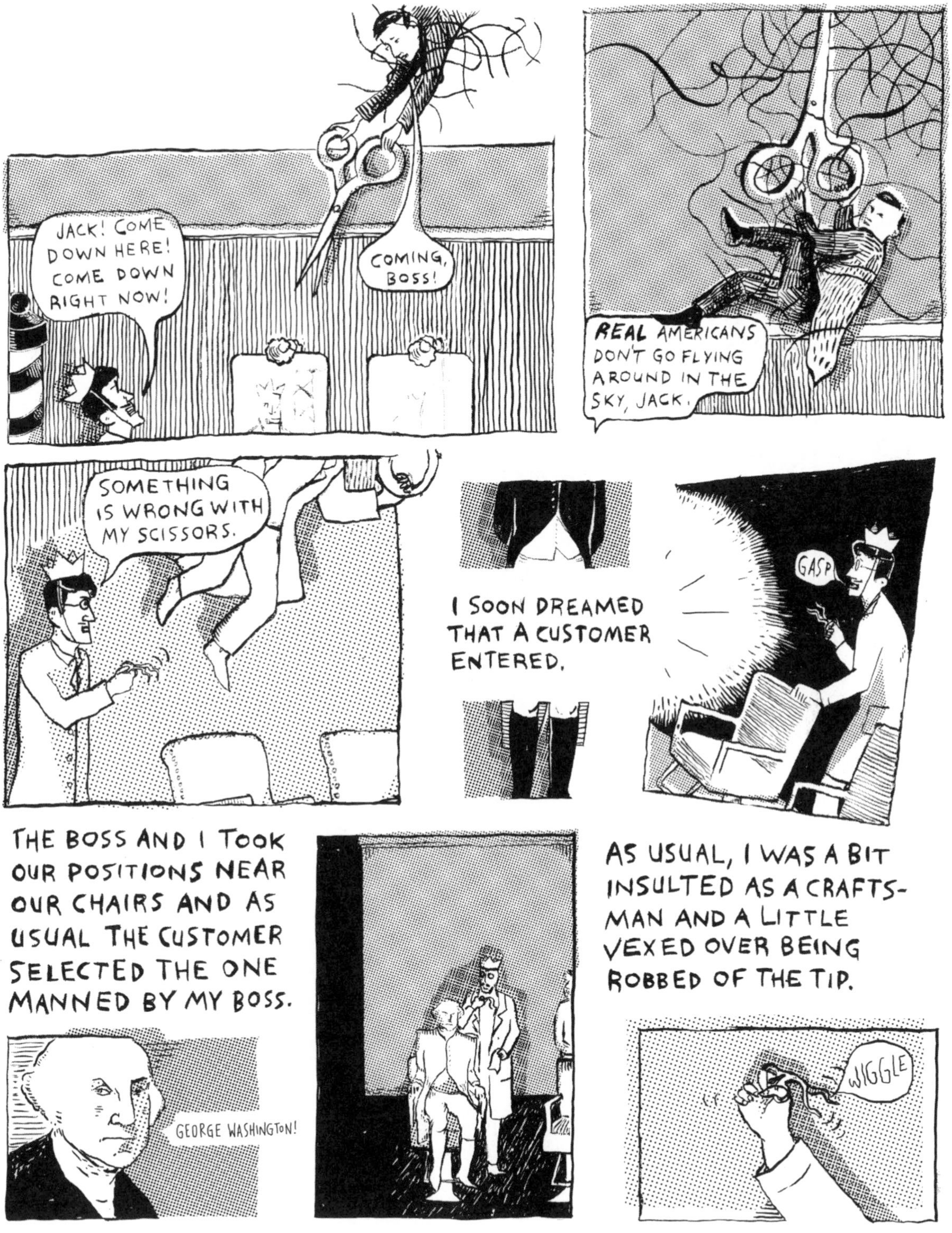
JACK! COME DOWN HERE! COME DOWN RIGHT NOW!
COMING, BOSS!
REAL AMERICANS DON'T GO FLYING AROUND IN THE SKY, JACK.
SOMETHING IS WRONG WITH MY SCISSORS.
I SOON DREAMED THAT A CUSTOMER ENTERED.
GASP
THE BOSS AND I TOOK OUR POSITIONS NEAR OUR CHAIRS AND AS USUAL THE CUSTOMER SELECTED THE ONE MANNED BY MY BOSS.
GEORGE WASHINGTON!
AS USUAL, I WAS A BIT INSULTED AS A CRAFTSMAN AND A LITTLE VEXED OVER BEING ROBBED OF THE TIP.
WIGGLE

BUT IT HAPPENED THAT THE BOSS WAS CALLED AWAY IN A HURRY AND HE ASKED ME TO TEND TO THE CUSTOMER.

I BEGAN TO WORK ON HIM, AND HE LAUGHED IN MY FACE.

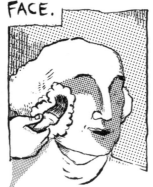

HE GRIMACED,

MADE FACES,

STUCK OUT HIS TONGUE,

AND BEGAN TO YELL.

AND THOUGH I DIDN'T UNDERSTAND THE LANGUAGE, I FELT HE WAS CALLING ME A CLUMSY BARBER.

MY PATIENCE FINALLY GAVE OUT.

AND AS I HELD THE RAZOR IN MY HAND (DON'T QUESTION A DREAM!), I SLIT HIS THROAT.

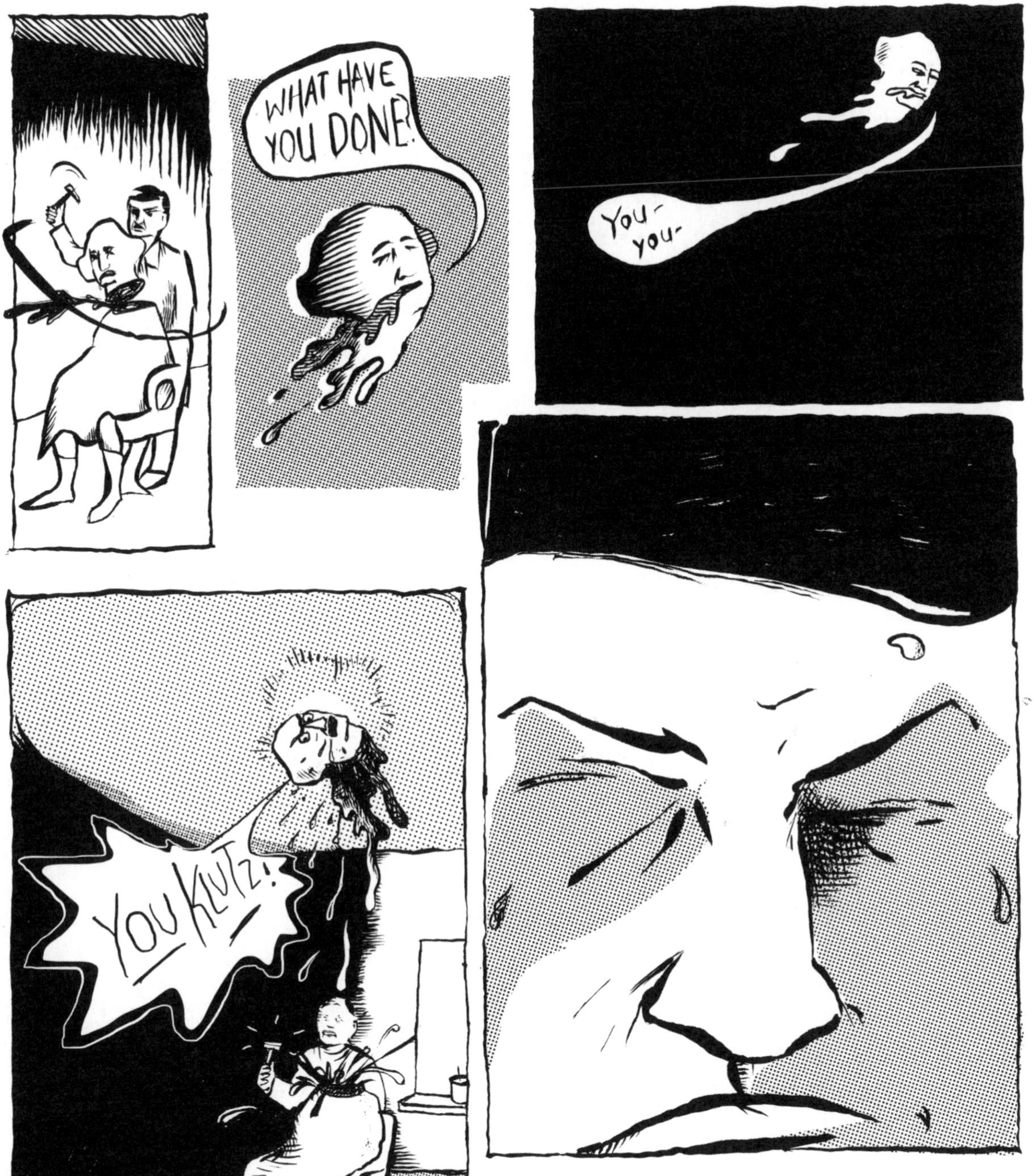
WHAT HAVE YOU DONE?
You- you-
YOU KLUTZ!

SO NATURALLY THERE WAS SCREAMING AND TUMULT AND I AWOKE.

I SPAT THREE TIMES TO BANISH MY DREAM, BUT IT DIDN'T HELP.

I TRIED STAYING HOME FROM WORK FOR TWO DAYS, BUT I CAN'T GET THE THOUGHTS OUT OF MY HEAD.

DEAR EDITOR,

IT MUST SEEM STRANGE, OR LIKE A STORY CREATED BY A SICK IMAGINATION, BUT WHAT I WRITE HERE IS THE TRUTH: SINCE MY FOOLISH DREAM, I CANNOT REST. I CAN'T FORGET THE SCENE. I AM ALWAYS LOST IN THOUGHT AND OBSESSED WITH THE DREAM. WHEN I STAND AT MY CHAIR AND HAVE TO USE MY RAZOR, I GET A SUDDEN IMPULSE TO DO WHAT I DID IN MY DREAM. THE GREATEST TEMPTATION I HAVE TO WITHSTAND IS WHEN MY RAZOR GETS UNDER THE CHIN CLOSE TO THE NECK. OH, THEN IT IS TERRIBLE!

I AM AFRAID I WILL GO MAD.

I HAVEN'T TOLD ANYONE ABOUT THIS YET, BECAUSE I AM ASHAMED. I BEG YOU TO ADVISE ME WHAT TO DO. SHALL I GIVE UP MY JOB? I AM WILLING TO DO ANYTHING TO RID MYSELF OF MY DILEMMA AND MY SUFFERING. I BEG YOU TO GIVE ME YOUR OPINION. ISN'T IT MADNESS?

—A MAD(?) BARBER

Man's thoughts often weave automatically through "idea-patterns," as they are called in psychological science, and the muscles respond automatically to the ideas. Every man with a healthy will can shake off the unwanted ideas and the reflexes they call forth to the muscles.

Every man can dream he commits a terrible crime, because in dreams the controllable will is slumbering. The writer of this letter must simply laugh off the dream and drive the whole matter out of his head. But if his nervous system is for some reason weakened and therefore his control over his willpower is likewise weak, he must consult a doctor. But he himself must be strong and overcome his impulse.

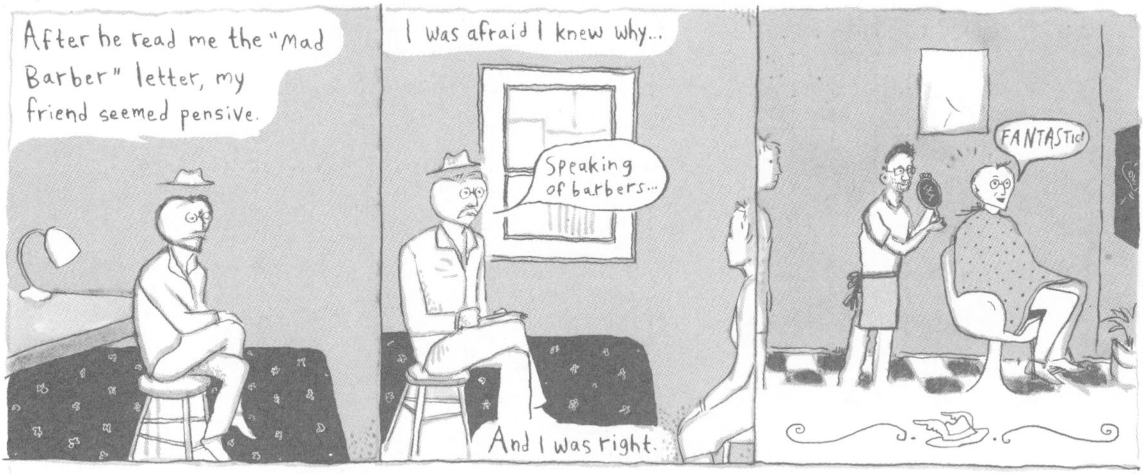
After he read me the "Mad Barber" letter, my friend seemed pensive.
I was afraid I knew why...
Speaking of barbers...
And I was right.
FANTASTIC!

After the haircut and shave, we walked through Times Square, the most crowded and tourist-filled part of the city. Cahan added to the hubbub by quoting Shakespeare:

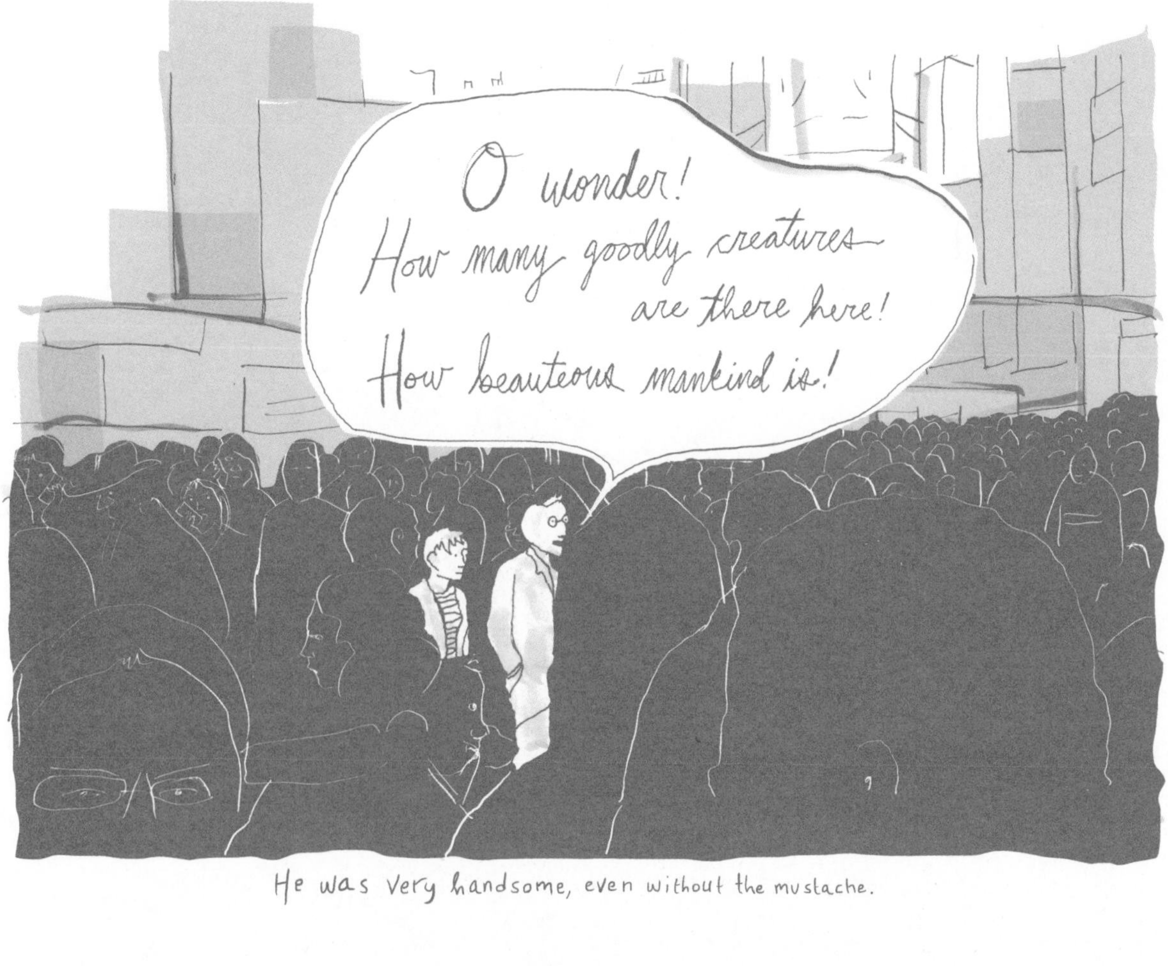
O wonder!
How many goodly creatures are there here!
How beauteous mankind is!

He was very handsome, even without the mustache.

5

FORMER
ASSISTANT DETECTIVE

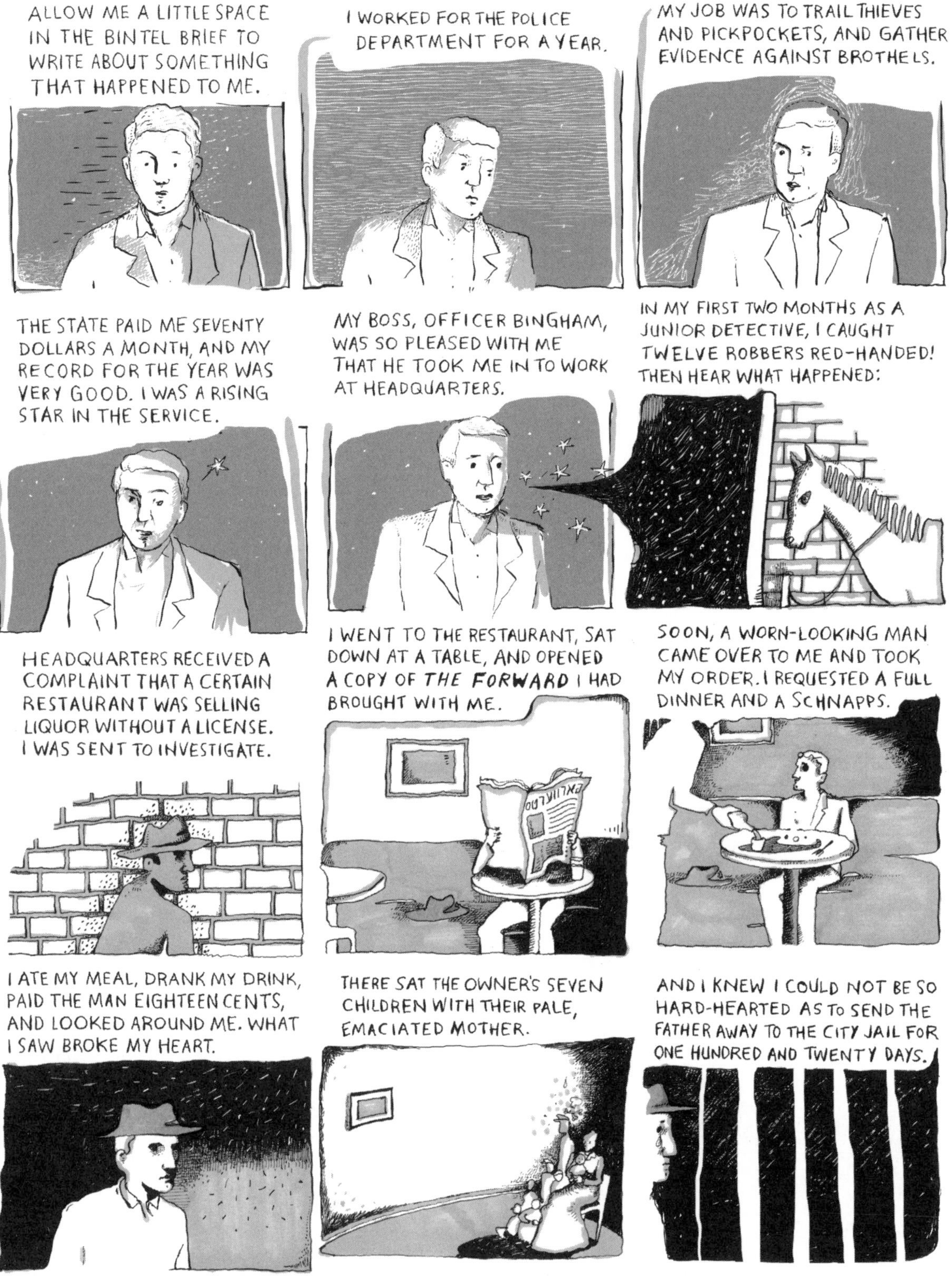
ALLOW ME A LITTLE SPACE IN THE BINTEL BRIEF TO WRITE ABOUT SOMETHING THAT HAPPENED TO ME.
I WORKED FOR THE POLICE DEPARTMENT FOR A YEAR.
MY JOB WAS TO TRAIL THIEVES AND PICKPOCKETS, AND GATHER EVIDENCE AGAINST BROTHELS.
THE STATE PAID ME SEVENTY DOLLARS A MONTH, AND MY RECORD FOR THE YEAR WAS VERY GOOD. I WAS A RISING STAR IN THE SERVICE.
MY BOSS, OFFICER BINGHAM, WAS SO PLEASED WITH ME THAT HE TOOK ME IN TO WORK AT HEADQUARTERS.
IN MY FIRST TWO MONTHS AS A JUNIOR DETECTIVE, I CAUGHT TWELVE ROBBERS RED-HANDED! THEN HEAR WHAT HAPPENED:
HEADQUARTERS RECEIVED A COMPLAINT THAT A CERTAIN RESTAURANT WAS SELLING LIQUOR WITHOUT A LICENSE. I WAS SENT TO INVESTIGATE.
I WENT TO THE RESTAURANT, SAT DOWN AT A TABLE, AND OPENED A COPY OF *THE FORWARD* I HAD BROUGHT WITH ME.
SOON, A WORN-LOOKING MAN CAME OVER TO ME AND TOOK MY ORDER. I REQUESTED A FULL DINNER AND A SCHNAPPS.
I ATE MY MEAL, DRANK MY DRINK, PAID THE MAN EIGHTEEN CENTS, AND LOOKED AROUND ME. WHAT I SAW BROKE MY HEART.
THERE SAT THE OWNER'S SEVEN CHILDREN WITH THEIR PALE, EMACIATED MOTHER.
AND I KNEW I COULD NOT BE SO HARD-HEARTED AS TO SEND THE FATHER AWAY TO THE CITY JAIL FOR ONE HUNDRED AND TWENTY DAYS.

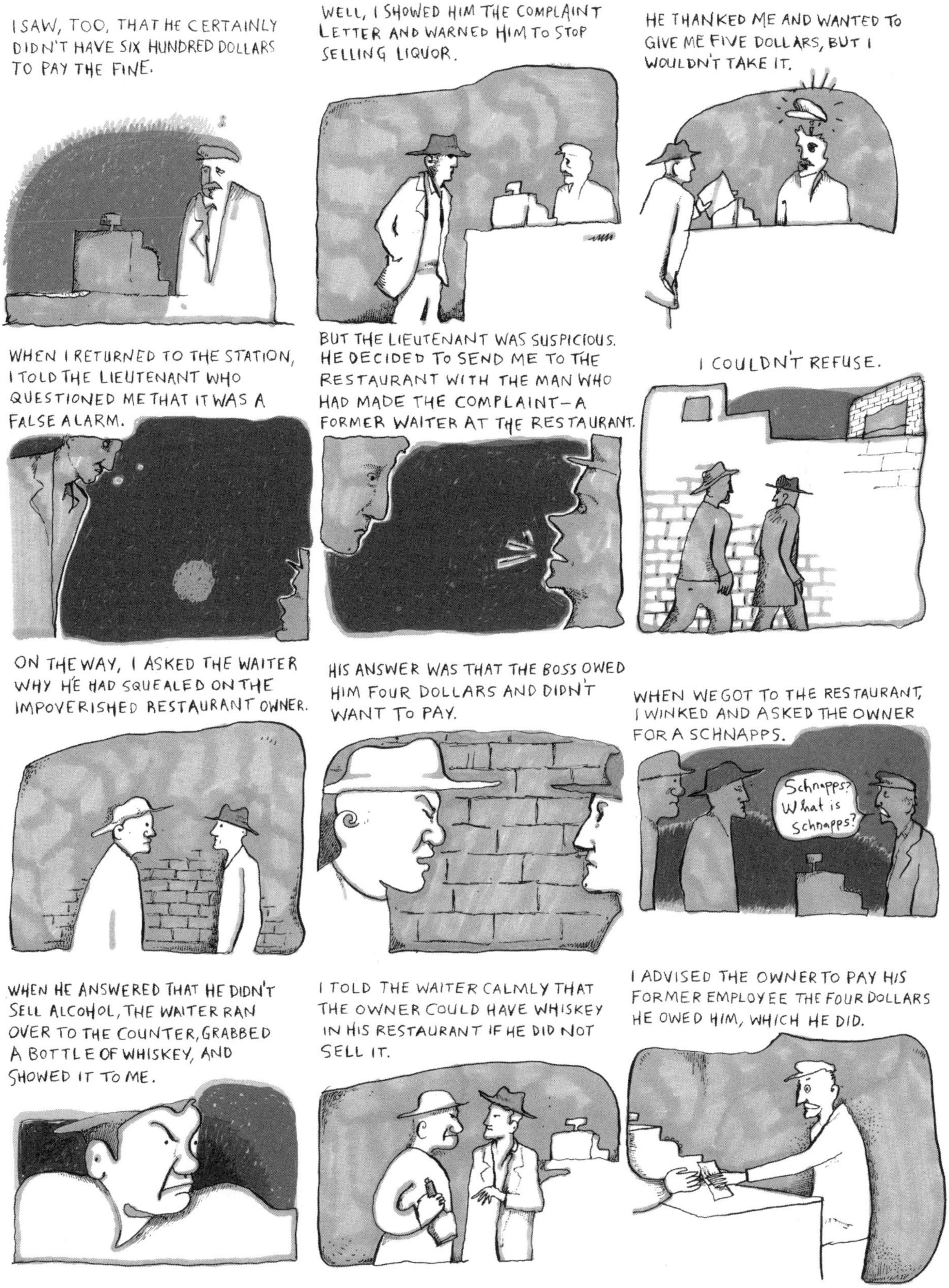
I SAW, TOO, THAT HE CERTAINLY DIDN'T HAVE SIX HUNDRED DOLLARS TO PAY THE FINE.
WELL, I SHOWED HIM THE COMPLAINT LETTER AND WARNED HIM TO STOP SELLING LIQUOR.
HE THANKED ME AND WANTED TO GIVE ME FIVE DOLLARS, BUT I WOULDN'T TAKE IT.
WHEN I RETURNED TO THE STATION, I TOLD THE LIEUTENANT WHO QUESTIONED ME THAT IT WAS A FALSE ALARM.
BUT THE LIEUTENANT WAS SUSPICIOUS. HE DECIDED TO SEND ME TO THE RESTAURANT WITH THE MAN WHO HAD MADE THE COMPLAINT—A FORMER WAITER AT THE RESTAURANT.
I COULDN'T REFUSE.
ON THE WAY, I ASKED THE WAITER WHY HE'D HAD SQUEALED ON THE IMPOVERISHED RESTAURANT OWNER.
HIS ANSWER WAS THAT THE BOSS OWED HIM FOUR DOLLARS AND DIDN'T WANT TO PAY.
WHEN WE GOT TO THE RESTAURANT, I WINKED AND ASKED THE OWNER FOR A SCHNAPPS.
Schnapps? What is schnapps?
WHEN HE ANSWERED THAT HE DIDN'T SELL ALCOHOL, THE WAITER RAN OVER TO THE COUNTER, GRABBED A BOTTLE OF WHISKEY, AND SHOWED IT TO ME.
I TOLD THE WAITER CALMLY THAT THE OWNER COULD HAVE WHISKEY IN HIS RESTAURANT IF HE DID NOT SELL IT.
I ADVISED THE OWNER TO PAY HIS FORMER EMPLOYEE THE FOUR DOLLARS HE OWED HIM, WHICH HE DID.

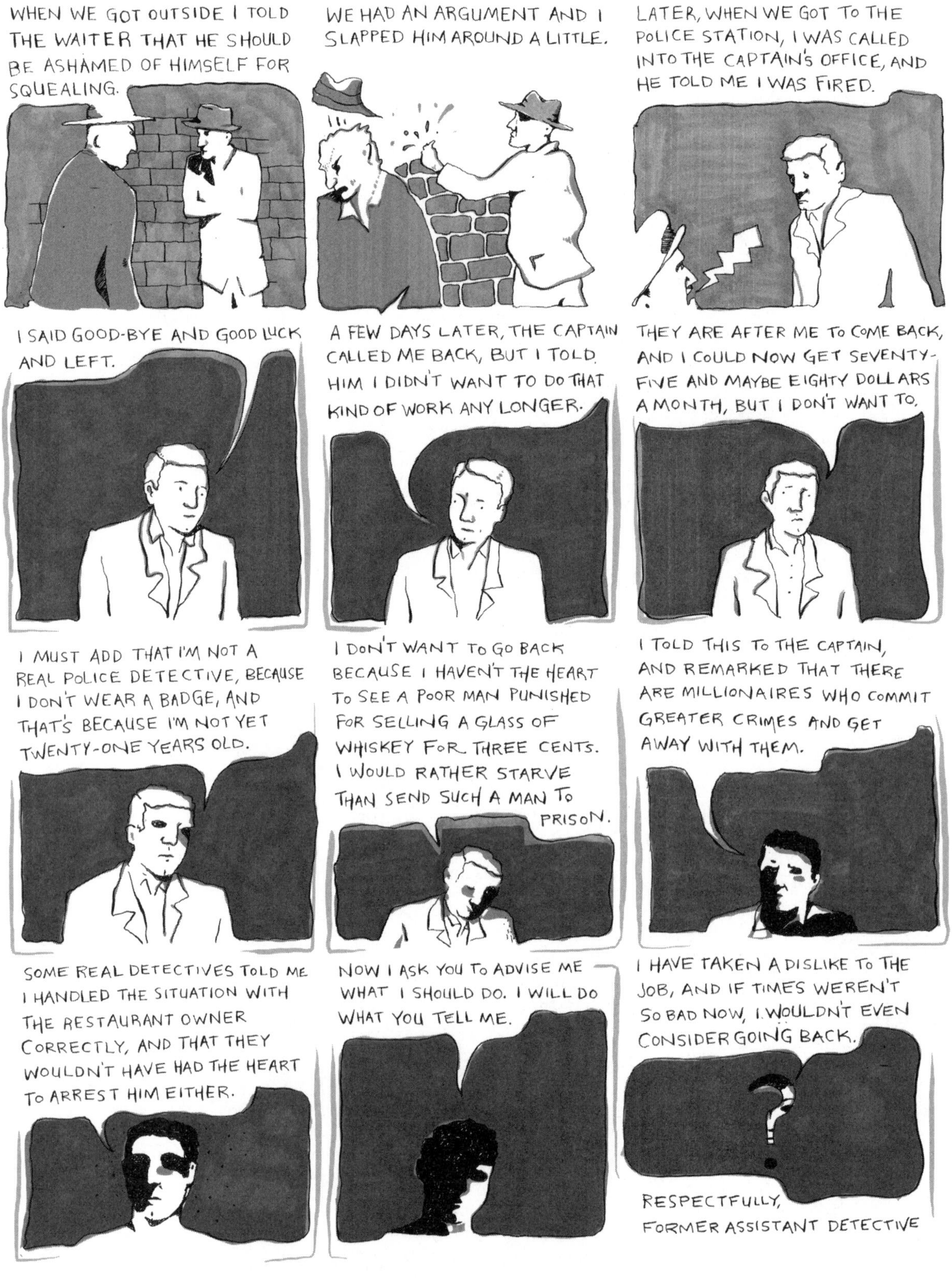
WHEN WE GOT OUTSIDE I TOLD THE WAITER THAT HE SHOULD BE ASHAMED OF HIMSELF FOR SQUEALING.
WE HAD AN ARGUMENT AND I SLAPPED HIM AROUND A LITTLE.
LATER, WHEN WE GOT TO THE POLICE STATION, I WAS CALLED INTO THE CAPTAIN'S OFFICE, AND HE TOLD ME I WAS FIRED.
I SAID GOOD-BYE AND GOOD LUCK AND LEFT.
A FEW DAYS LATER, THE CAPTAIN CALLED ME BACK, BUT I TOLD HIM I DIDN'T WANT TO DO THAT KIND OF WORK ANY LONGER.
THEY ARE AFTER ME TO COME BACK, AND I COULD NOW GET SEVENTY-FIVE AND MAYBE EIGHTY DOLLARS A MONTH, BUT I DON'T WANT TO.
I MUST ADD THAT I'M NOT A REAL POLICE DETECTIVE, BECAUSE I DON'T WEAR A BADGE, AND THAT'S BECAUSE I'M NOT YET TWENTY-ONE YEARS OLD.
I DON'T WANT TO GO BACK BECAUSE I HAVEN'T THE HEART TO SEE A POOR MAN PUNISHED FOR SELLING A GLASS OF WHISKEY FOR THREE CENTS. I WOULD RATHER STARVE THAN SEND SUCH A MAN TO PRISON.
I TOLD THIS TO THE CAPTAIN, AND REMARKED THAT THERE ARE MILLIONAIRES WHO COMMIT GREATER CRIMES AND GET AWAY WITH THEM.
SOME REAL DETECTIVES TOLD ME I HANDLED THE SITUATION WITH THE RESTAURANT OWNER CORRECTLY, AND THAT THEY WOULDN'T HAVE HAD THE HEART TO ARREST HIM EITHER.
NOW I ASK YOU TO ADVISE ME WHAT I SHOULD DO. I WILL DO WHAT YOU TELL ME.
I HAVE TAKEN A DISLIKE TO THE JOB, AND IF TIMES WEREN'T SO BAD NOW, I WOULDN'T EVEN CONSIDER GOING BACK.
RESPECTFULLY,
FORMER ASSISTANT DETECTIVE

In the answer, the young assistant detective is praised for not wanting to inform on a poor man. Our advice to him is to run from the job as from a fire, because this work is not fit for such a fine, kindhearted young man. It is not right to place himself in servitude to the Police Department. There is the danger that he might, in time, not be able to withstand temptation and it would be hard to guard himself against sinking into the corruption of immoral police practices.

SCHNAPPS

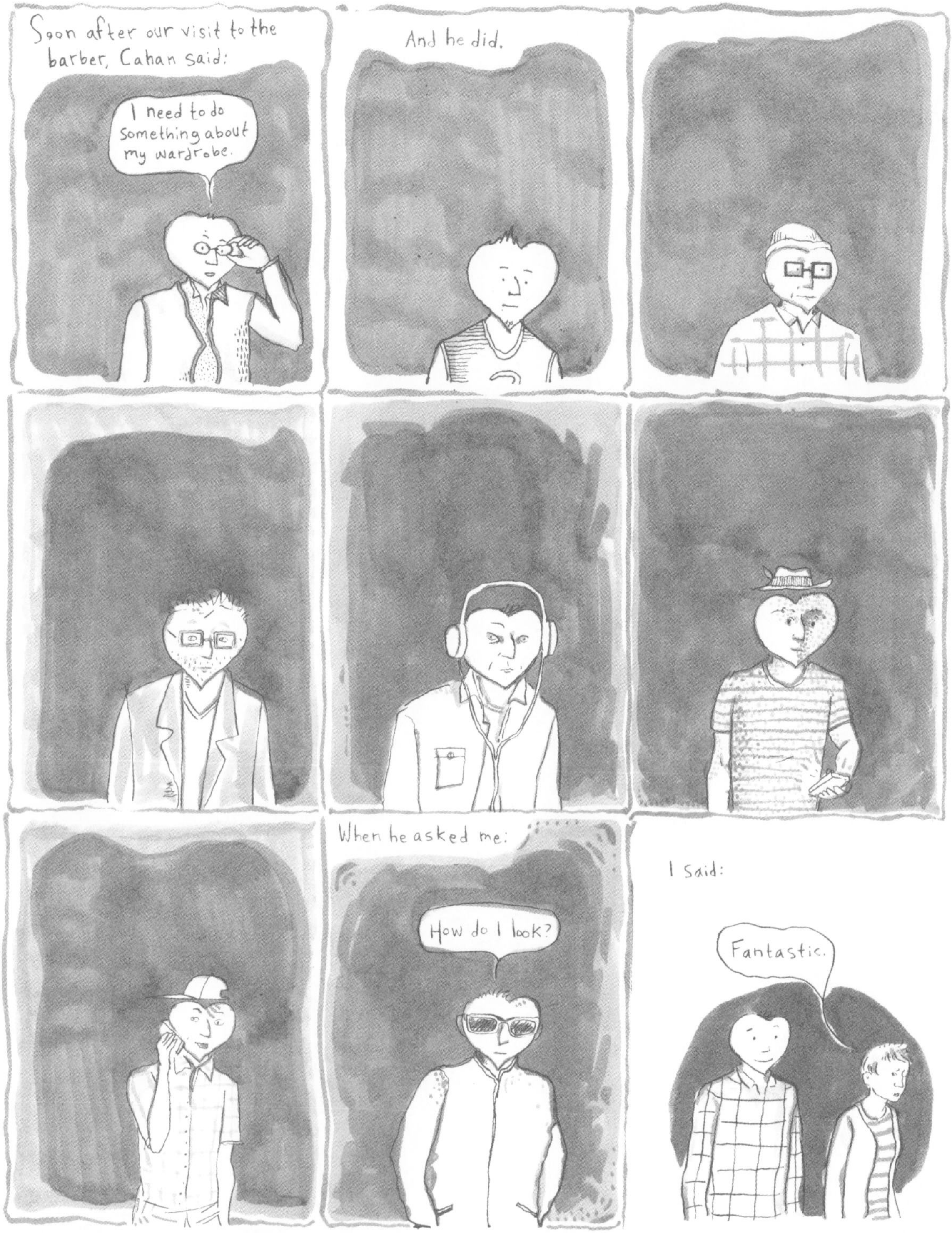
Soon after our visit to the barber, Cahan said:
I need to do something about my wardrobe.
And he did.
When he asked me:
How do I look?
I said:
Fantastic.

6

THE BRIDEGROOM

WORTHY EDITOR,

I WAS BORN IN AMERICA AND MY PARENTS GAVE ME A GOOD EDUCATION.

I STUDIED YIDDISH AND HEBREW AND GRADUATED FROM HIGH SCHOOL WITH HONORS. AFTER THAT, I TOOK A COURSE IN BOOKKEEPING AND GOT A GOOD JOB.

I HAD MANY FRIENDS, AND SEVERAL BOYS PROPOSED TO ME. BUT I WASN'T READY.

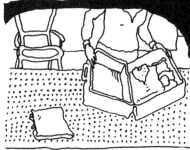

INSTEAD, I WENT TO VISIT MY PARENTS' HOMETOWN IN RUSSIAN POLAND.

MY MOTHER'S YOUNGER SISTER WAS GETTING MARRIED. MY PARENTS COULDN'T GO TO THE WEDDING, SO THEY SENT ME INSTEAD.

I SAILED ON A FIRST-CLASS TICKET.

MY AUNT, MY UNCLE AND MY GRANDMOTHER WELCOMED ME WITH TEARS OF JOY. I STAYED WITH THEM SIX MONTHS AND LACKED FOR NOTHING.

IT WAS LIVELY IN THE TOWN.

I WAS ACCEPTED WARMLY INTO ALL THE ORGANIZATIONS AND CLUBS. AFTER ALL, I WAS A CITIZEN OF THE "GOLDEN LAND."

AMONG THE SOCIAL LEADERS OF THE COMMUNITY WAS AN INTELLIGENT YOUNG MAN, A FRIEND OF MY UNCLE'S WHO TOOK ME TO VARIOUS GATHERINGS.

ONE DAY, HE DECLARED HIS LOVE FOR ME IN A BEAUTIFUL LETTER.

HIS PROPOSAL DID NOT TAKE ME ENTIRELY BY SURPRISE. STILL, IT WORRIED ME. HE WAS NOT THE MAN I HAD IMAGINED FOR MYSELF.

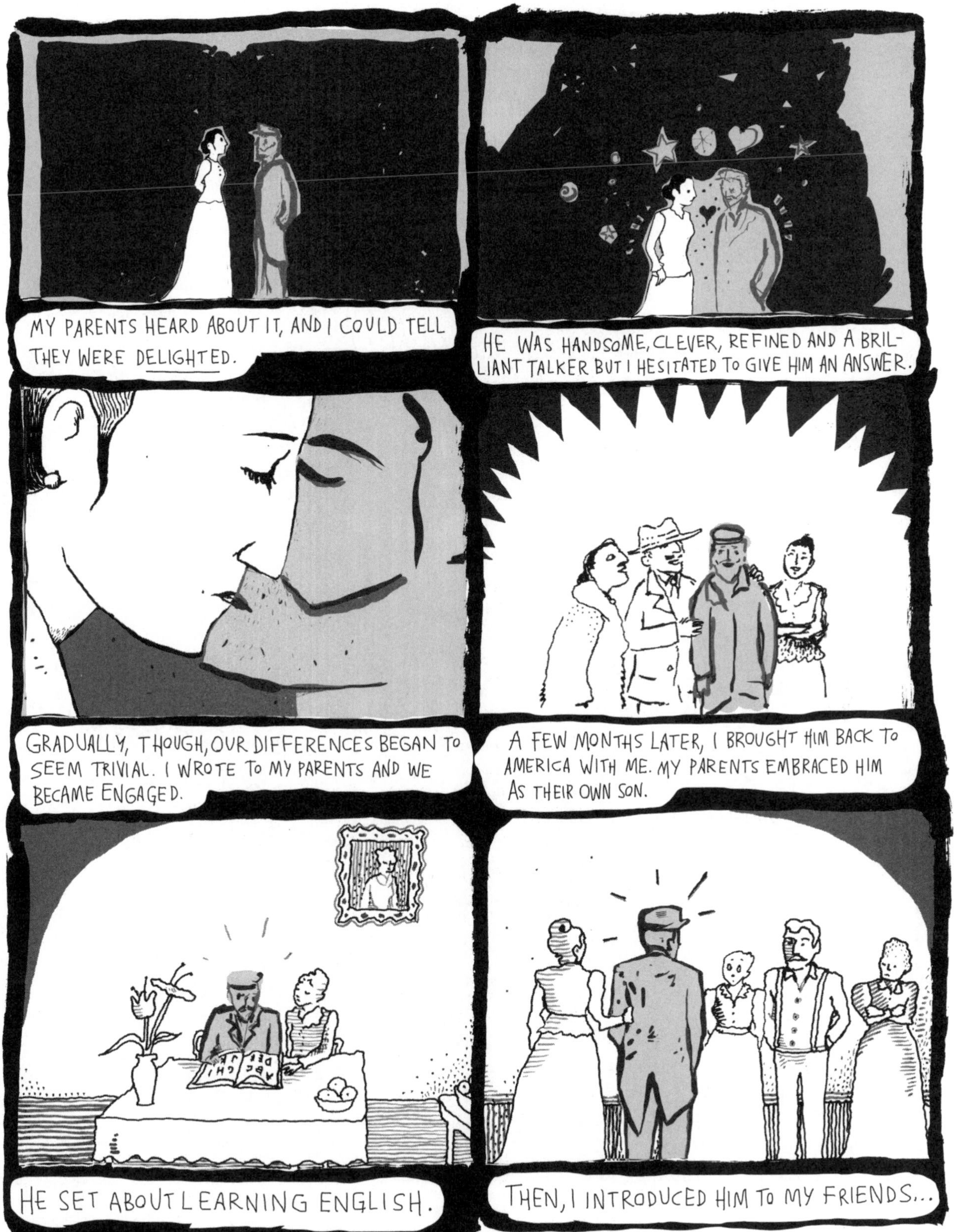
MY PARENTS HEARD ABOUT IT, AND I COULD TELL THEY WERE DELIGHTED.
HE WAS HANDSOME, CLEVER, REFINED AND A BRILLIANT TALKER BUT I HESITATED TO GIVE HIM AN ANSWER.
GRADUALLY, THOUGH, OUR DIFFERENCES BEGAN TO SEEM TRIVIAL. I WROTE TO MY PARENTS AND WE BECAME ENGAGED.
A FEW MONTHS LATER, I BROUGHT HIM BACK TO AMERICA WITH ME. MY PARENTS EMBRACED HIM AS THEIR OWN SON.
HE SET ABOUT LEARNING ENGLISH.
THEN, I INTRODUCED HIM TO MY FRIENDS...

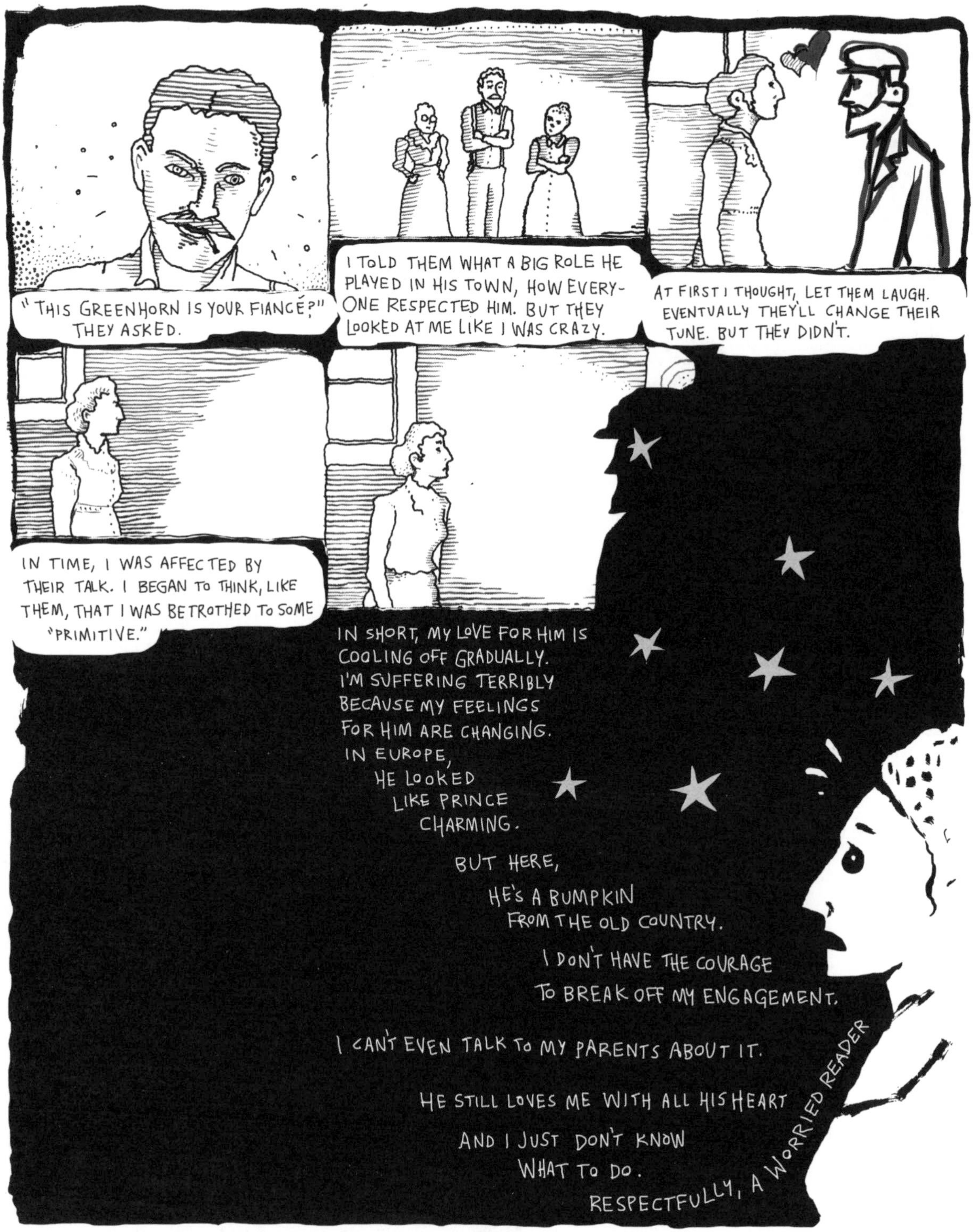
"THIS GREENHORN IS YOUR FIANCÉ?" THEY ASKED.
I TOLD THEM WHAT A BIG ROLE HE PLAYED IN HIS TOWN, HOW EVERYONE RESPECTED HIM. BUT THEY LOOKED AT ME LIKE I WAS CRAZY.
AT FIRST I THOUGHT, LET THEM LAUGH. EVENTUALLY THEY'LL CHANGE THEIR TUNE. BUT THEY DIDN'T.
IN TIME, I WAS AFFECTED BY THEIR TALK. I BEGAN TO THINK, LIKE THEM, THAT I WAS BETROTHED TO SOME "PRIMITIVE."
IN SHORT, MY LOVE FOR HIM IS COOLING OFF GRADUALLY. I'M SUFFERING TERRIBLY BECAUSE MY FEELINGS FOR HIM ARE CHANGING. IN EUROPE, HE LOOKED LIKE PRINCE CHARMING.
BUT HERE, HE'S A BUMPKIN FROM THE OLD COUNTRY.
I DON'T HAVE THE COURAGE TO BREAK OFF MY ENGAGEMENT.
I CAN'T EVEN TALK TO MY PARENTS ABOUT IT.
HE STILL LOVES ME WITH ALL HIS HEART AND I JUST DON'T KNOW WHAT TO DO.
RESPECTFULLY, A WORRIED READER

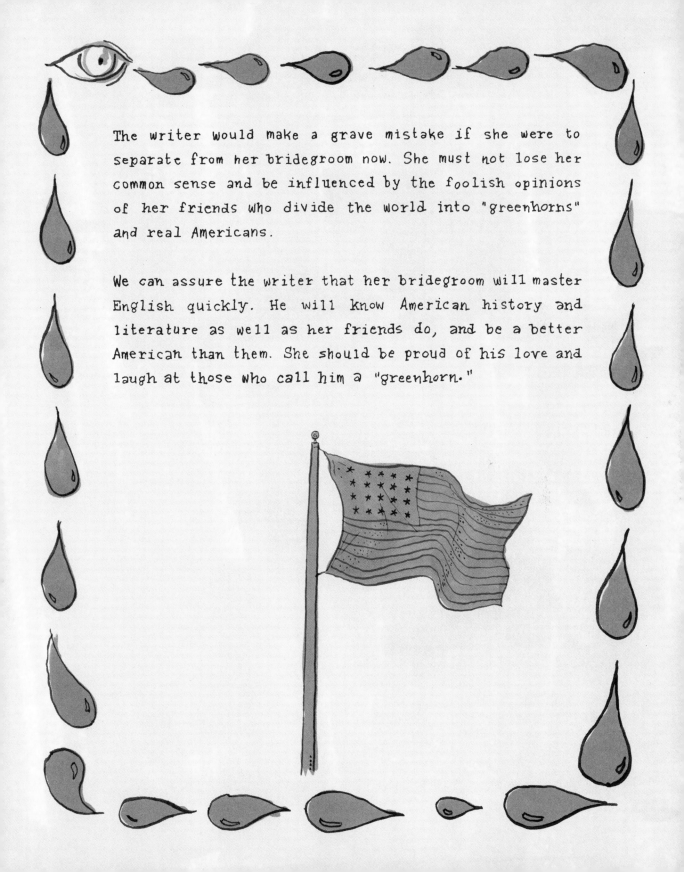

The writer would make a grave mistake if she were to separate from her bridegroom now. She must not lose her common sense and be influenced by the foolish opinions of her friends who divide the world into "greenhorns" and real Americans.

We can assure the writer that her bridegroom will master English quickly. He will know American history and literature as well as her friends do, and be a better American than them. She should be proud of his love and laugh at those who call him a "greenhorn."

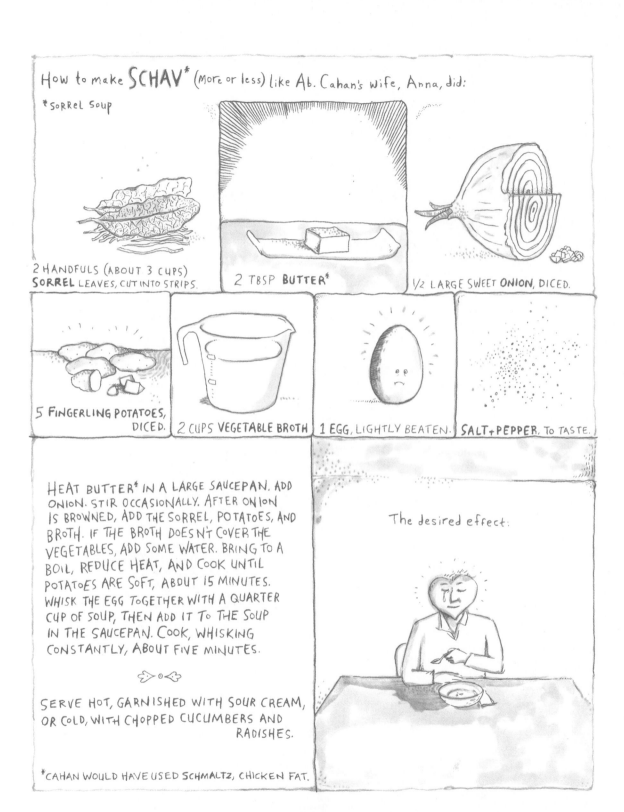

How to make **SCHAV*** (more or less) like Ab. Cahan's wife, Anna, did:

*Sorrel Soup

2 HANDFULS (ABOUT 3 CUPS) **SORREL** LEAVES, CUT INTO STRIPS.

2 TBSP **BUTTER***

1/2 LARGE SWEET **ONION**, DICED.

5 **FINGERLING POTATOES**, DICED.

2 CUPS **VEGETABLE BROTH**

1 **EGG**, LIGHTLY BEATEN.

SALT+PEPPER, TO TASTE.

HEAT BUTTER* IN A LARGE SAUCEPAN. ADD ONION. STIR OCCASIONALLY. AFTER ONION IS BROWNED, ADD THE SORREL, POTATOES, AND BROTH. IF THE BROTH DOESN'T COVER THE VEGETABLES, ADD SOME WATER. BRING TO A BOIL, REDUCE HEAT, AND COOK UNTIL POTATOES ARE SOFT, ABOUT 15 MINUTES. WHISK THE EGG TOGETHER WITH A QUARTER CUP OF SOUP, THEN ADD IT TO THE SOUP IN THE SAUCEPAN. COOK, WHISKING CONSTANTLY, ABOUT FIVE MINUTES.

SERVE HOT, GARNISHED WITH SOUR CREAM, OR COLD, WITH CHOPPED CUCUMBERS AND RADISHES.

The desired effect:

*CAHAN WOULD HAVE USED SCHMALTZ, CHICKEN FAT.

7

BORN OUT OF WEDLOCK

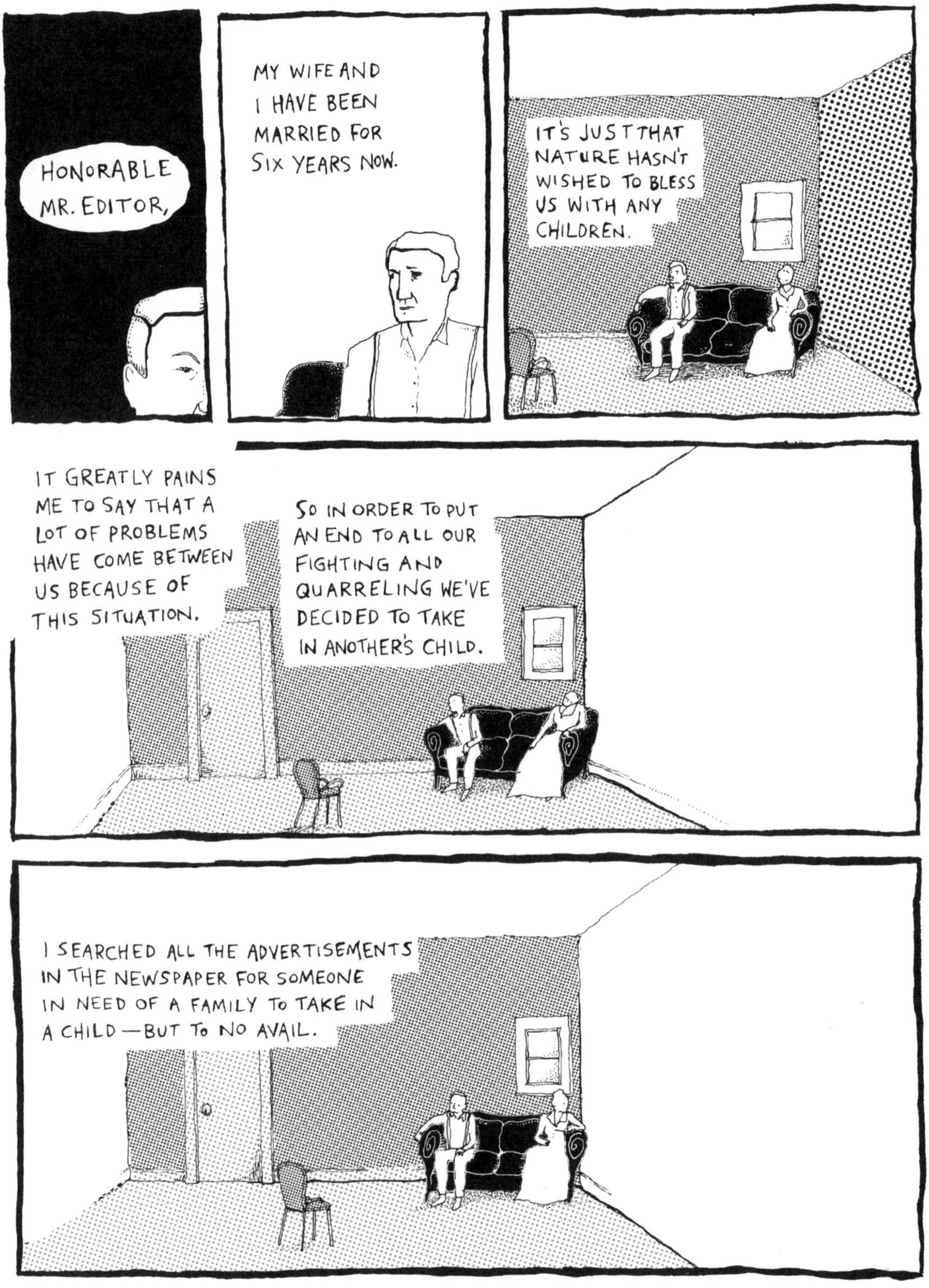
HONORABLE MR. EDITOR,
MY WIFE AND I HAVE BEEN MARRIED FOR SIX YEARS NOW.
IT'S JUST THAT NATURE HASN'T WISHED TO BLESS US WITH ANY CHILDREN.
IT GREATLY PAINS ME TO SAY THAT A LOT OF PROBLEMS HAVE COME BETWEEN US BECAUSE OF THIS SITUATION.
SO IN ORDER TO PUT AN END TO ALL OUR FIGHTING AND QUARRELING WE'VE DECIDED TO TAKE IN ANOTHER'S CHILD.
I SEARCHED ALL THE ADVERTISEMENTS IN THE NEWSPAPER FOR SOMEONE IN NEED OF A FAMILY TO TAKE IN A CHILD—BUT TO NO AVAIL.

THIS WEEK, HOWEVER, A COUNTRYMAN OF OURS CAME TO US AND TOLD US THAT A YOUNG LADY IN HIS HOUSE HAD AN ILLEGITIMATE CHILD AND THAT SHE WISHES TO "GIFT IT AWAY" TO A PROPER FAMILY.

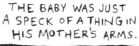

HE'S A FINE BOY, ONLY FOUR MONTHS OLD.

THE MOTHER IS A "GREENHORN" WITHOUT FRIENDS OR MONEY. SHE CAN'T PROVIDE FOR THE CHILD

I WOULD ADVISE YOU TO GO SEE THE BABY RIGHT AWAY. THE MOTHER CAN'T KEEP HIM MUCH LONGER, AND THIS IS THE KIND OF DECISION YOU SHOULDN'T THINK ABOUT TOO LONG.

THE BABY WAS JUST A SPECK OF A THING IN HIS MOTHER'S ARMS.

I HELD MY ARMS OUT,

AND SHE LET ME HOLD HIM FOR A MOMENT.

THANK YOU.

THEN I RAN HOME TO TALK THINGS OVER WITH MY WIFE.

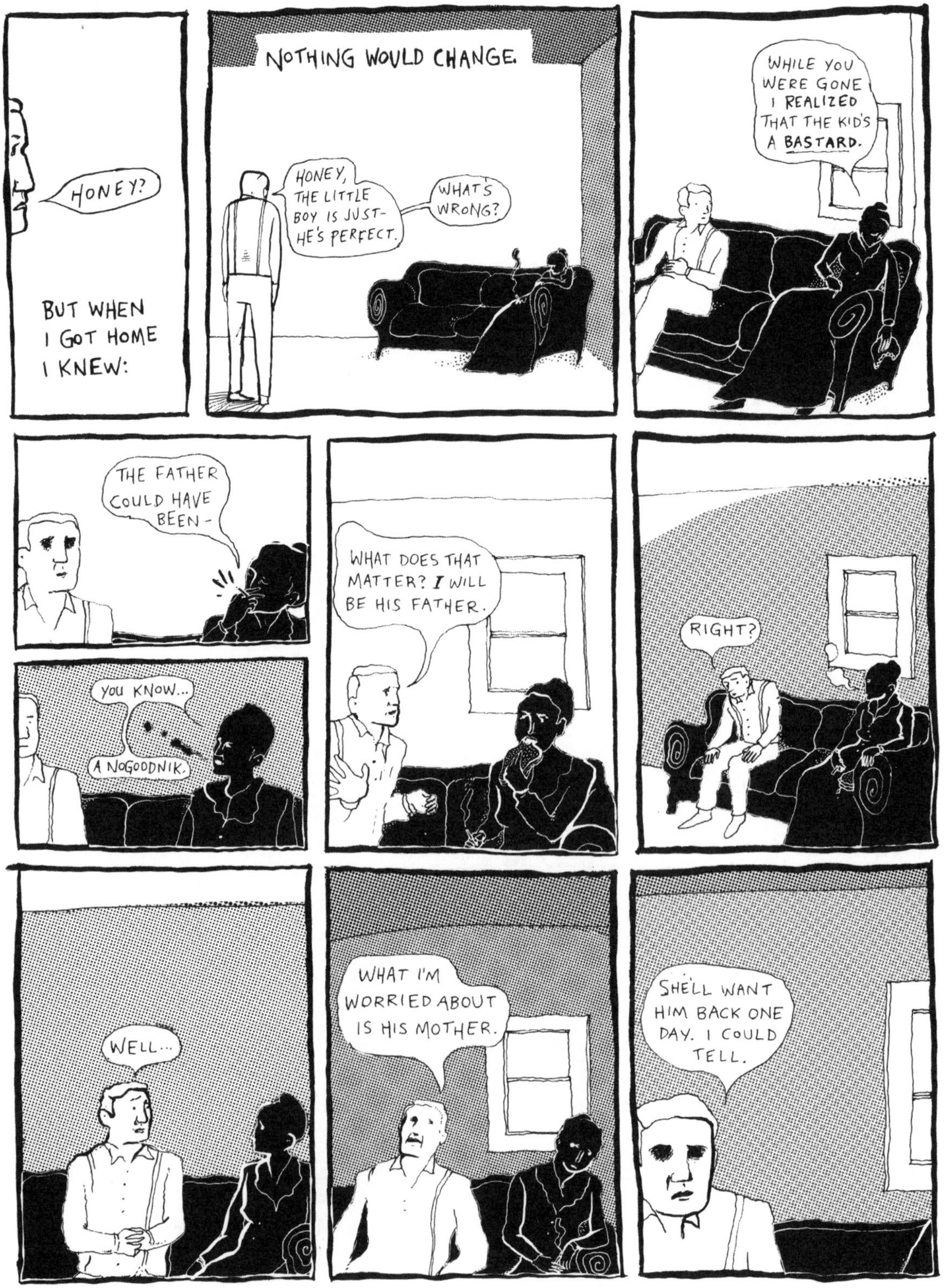

HONEY?
BUT WHEN I GOT HOME I KNEW:
NOTHING WOULD CHANGE.
HONEY, THE LITTLE BOY IS JUST- HE'S PERFECT.
WHAT'S WRONG?
WHILE YOU WERE GONE I REALIZED THAT THE KID'S A BASTARD.
THE FATHER COULD HAVE BEEN-
YOU KNOW...
A NOGOODNIK.
WHAT DOES THAT MATTER? I WILL BE HIS FATHER.
RIGHT?
WELL...
WHAT I'M WORRIED ABOUT IS HIS MOTHER.
SHE'LL WANT HIM BACK ONE DAY. I COULD TELL.

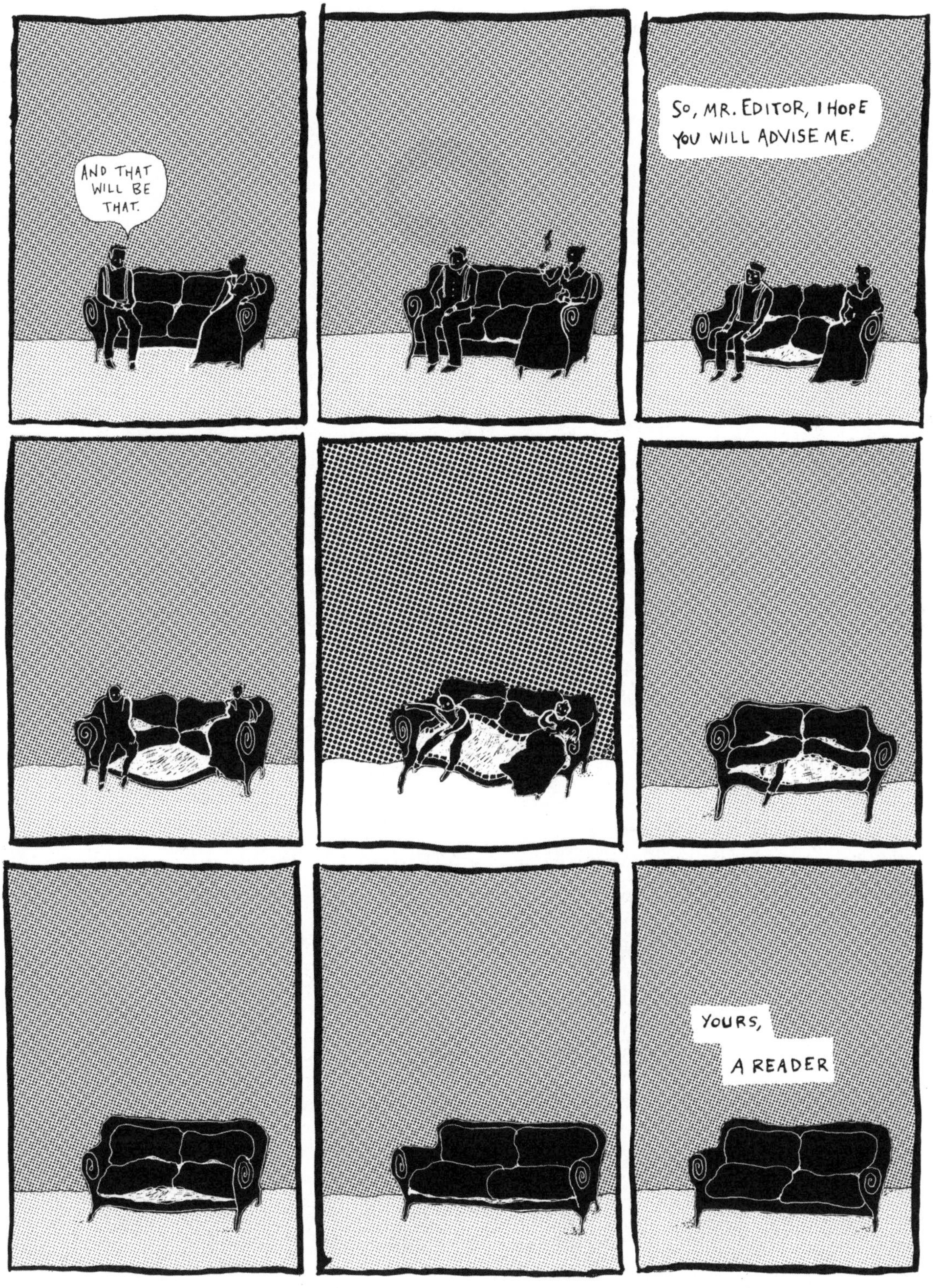
AND THAT WILL BE THAT.
SO, MR. EDITOR, I HOPE YOU WILL ADVISE ME.
YOURS,
A READER

You and your wife are letting yourselves fall into the trap of "Hamletism," which is to say that you are paralyzed by thinking too hard. You should stop asking "to be, or not to be," and adopt the child immediately.

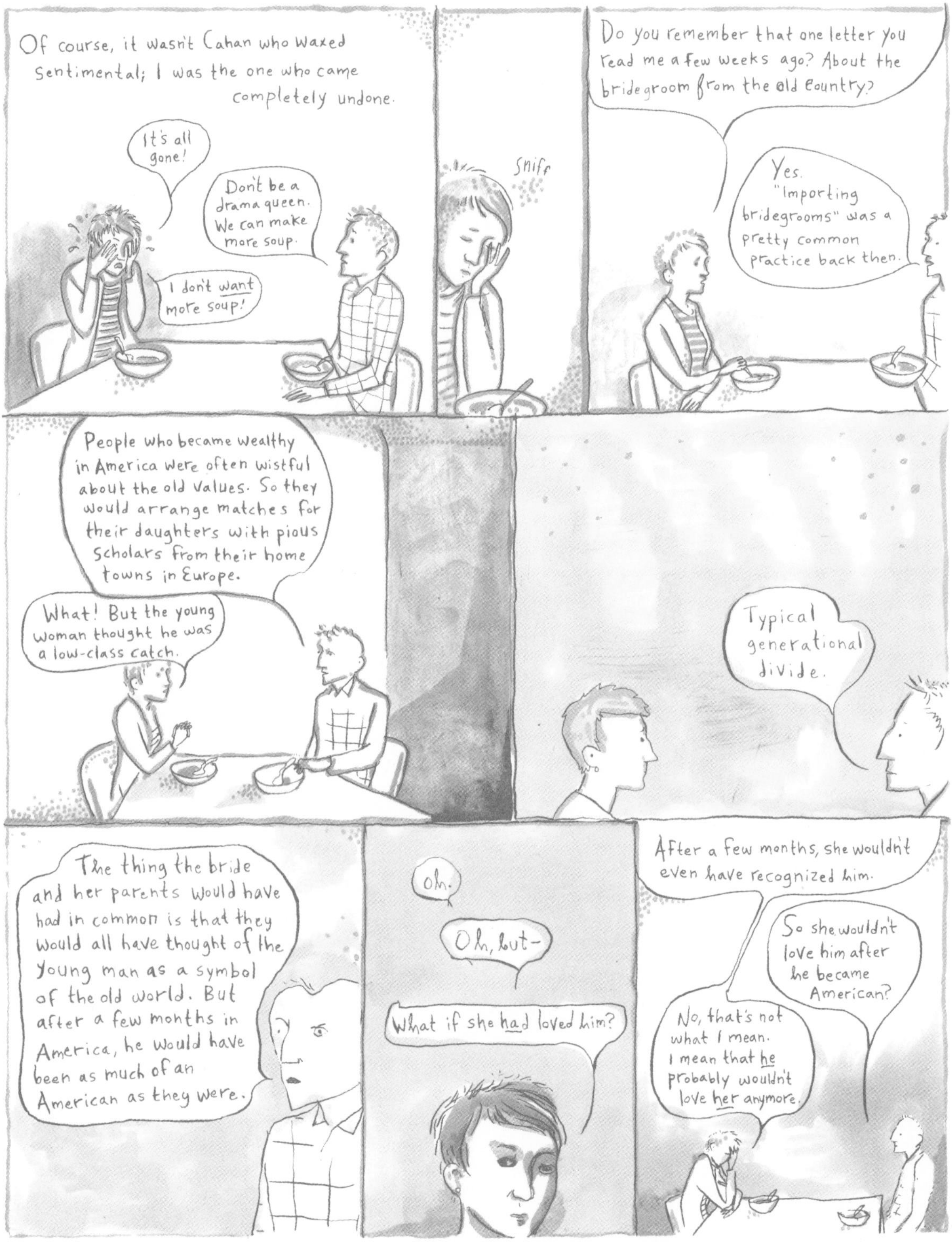
Of course, it wasn't Cahan who waxed sentimental; I was the one who came completely undone.
It's all gone!
Don't be a drama queen. We can make more soup.
I don't want more soup!
Sniff
Do you remember that one letter you read me a few weeks ago? About the bridegroom from the old country?
Yes. "Importing bridegrooms" was a pretty common practice back then.
People who became wealthy in America were often wistful about the old values. So they would arrange matches for their daughters with pious scholars from their home towns in Europe.
What! But the young woman thought he was a low-class catch.
Typical generational divide.
The thing the bride and her parents would have had in common is that they would all have thought of the young man as a symbol of the old world. But after a few months in America, he would have been as much of an American as they were.
Oh.
Oh, but-
What if she had loved him?
After a few months, she wouldn't even have recognized him.
So she wouldn't love him after he became American?
No, that's not what I mean. I mean that he probably wouldn't love her anymore.

8

THE TWO-TIMER

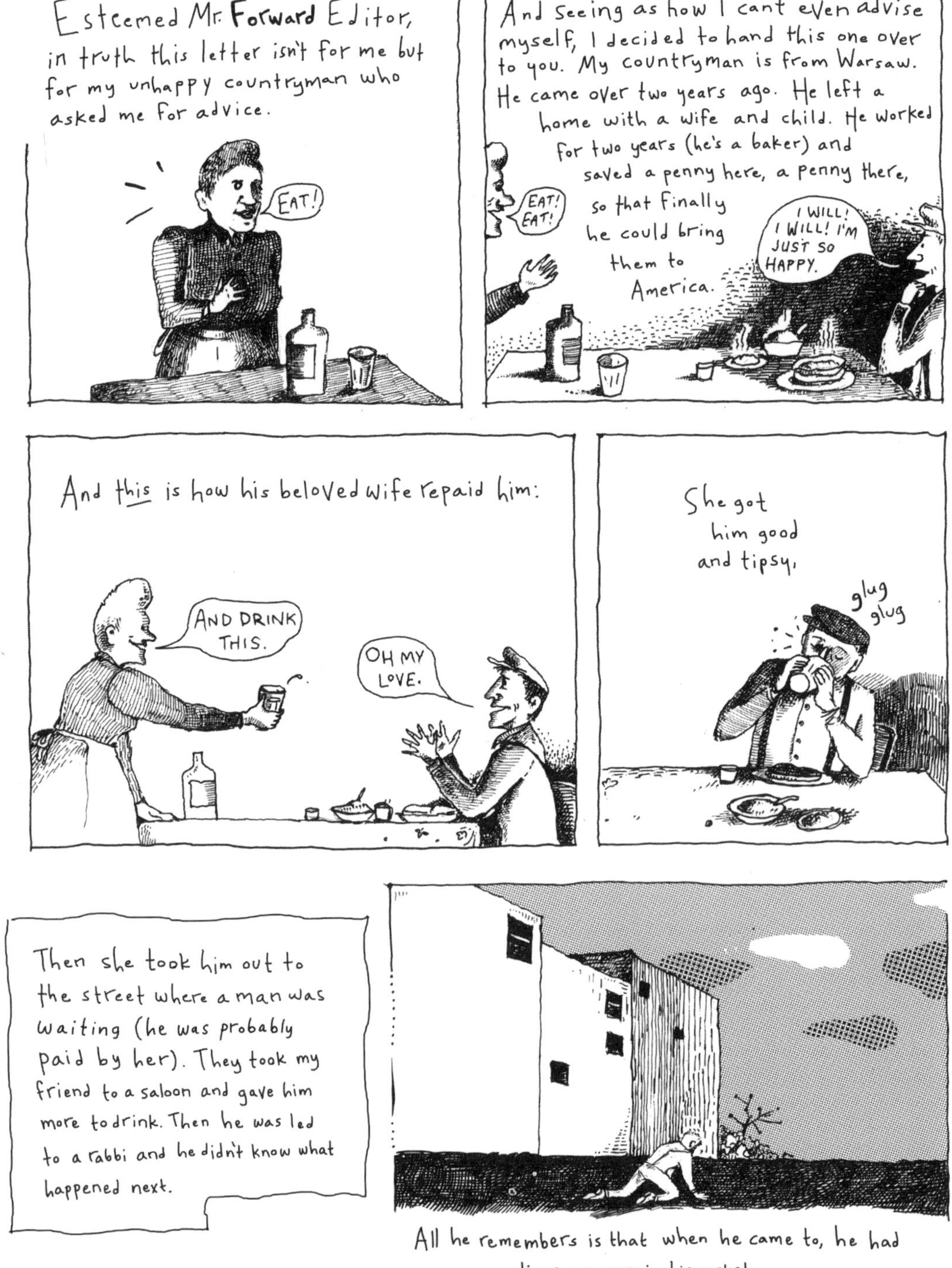
Esteemed Mr. Forward Editor, in truth this letter isn't for me but for my unhappy countryman who asked me for advice.
EAT!
And seeing as how I can't even advise myself, I decided to hand this one over to you. My countryman is from Warsaw. He came over two years ago. He left a home with a wife and child. He worked for two years (he's a baker) and saved a penny here, a penny there,
EAT! EAT!
so that finally he could bring them to America.
I WILL! I WILL! I'M JUST SO HAPPY.
And this is how his beloved wife repaid him:
AND DRINK THIS.
OH MY LOVE.
She got him good and tipsy,
glug glug
Then she took him out to the street where a man was waiting (he was probably paid by her). They took my friend to a saloon and gave him more to drink. Then he was led to a rabbi and he didn't know what happened next.
All he remembers is that when he came to, he had divorce papers in his pocket.

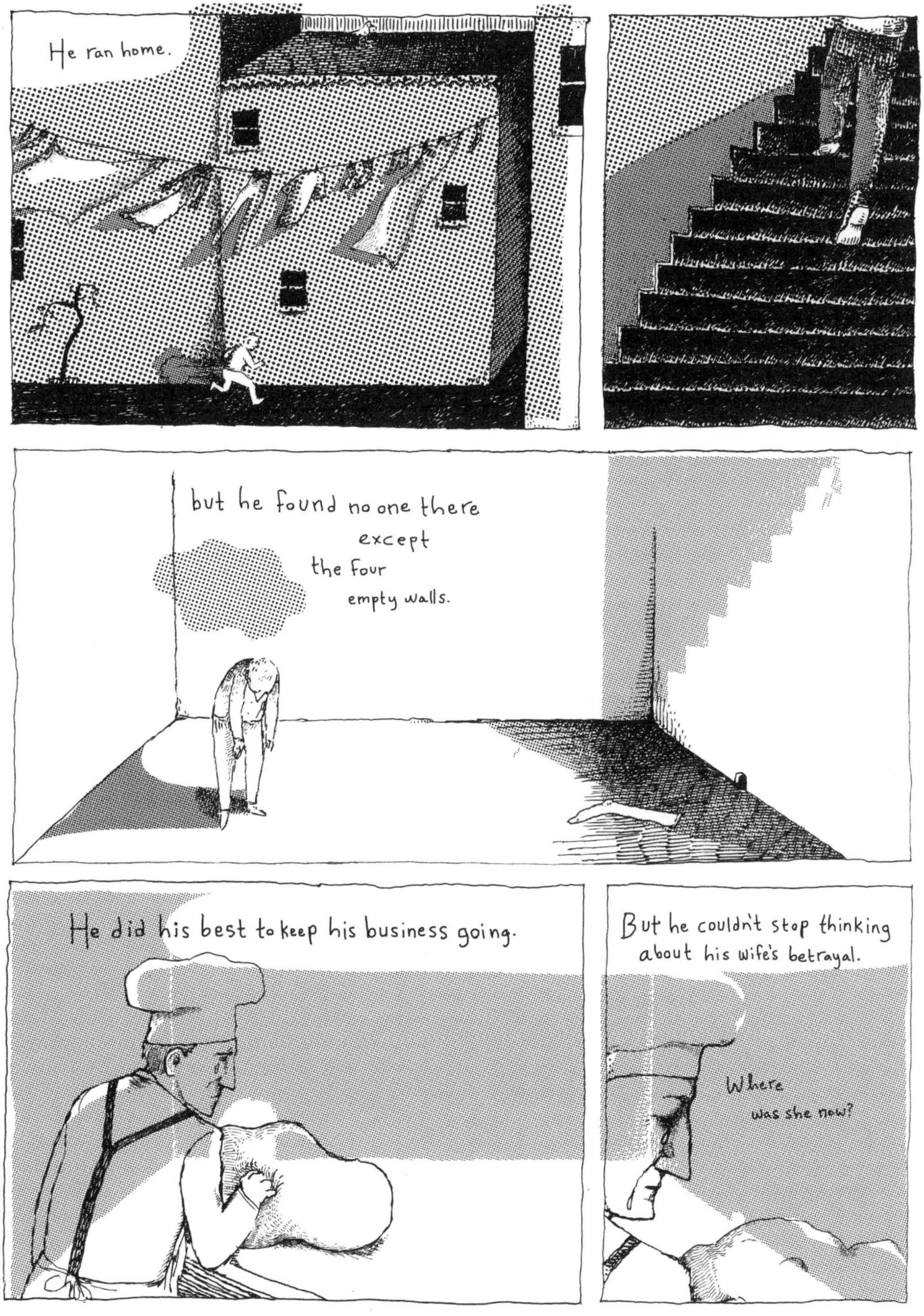
He ran home.
but he found no one there except the four empty walls.
He did his best to keep his business going.
But he couldn't stop thinking about his wife's betrayal.
Where was she now?

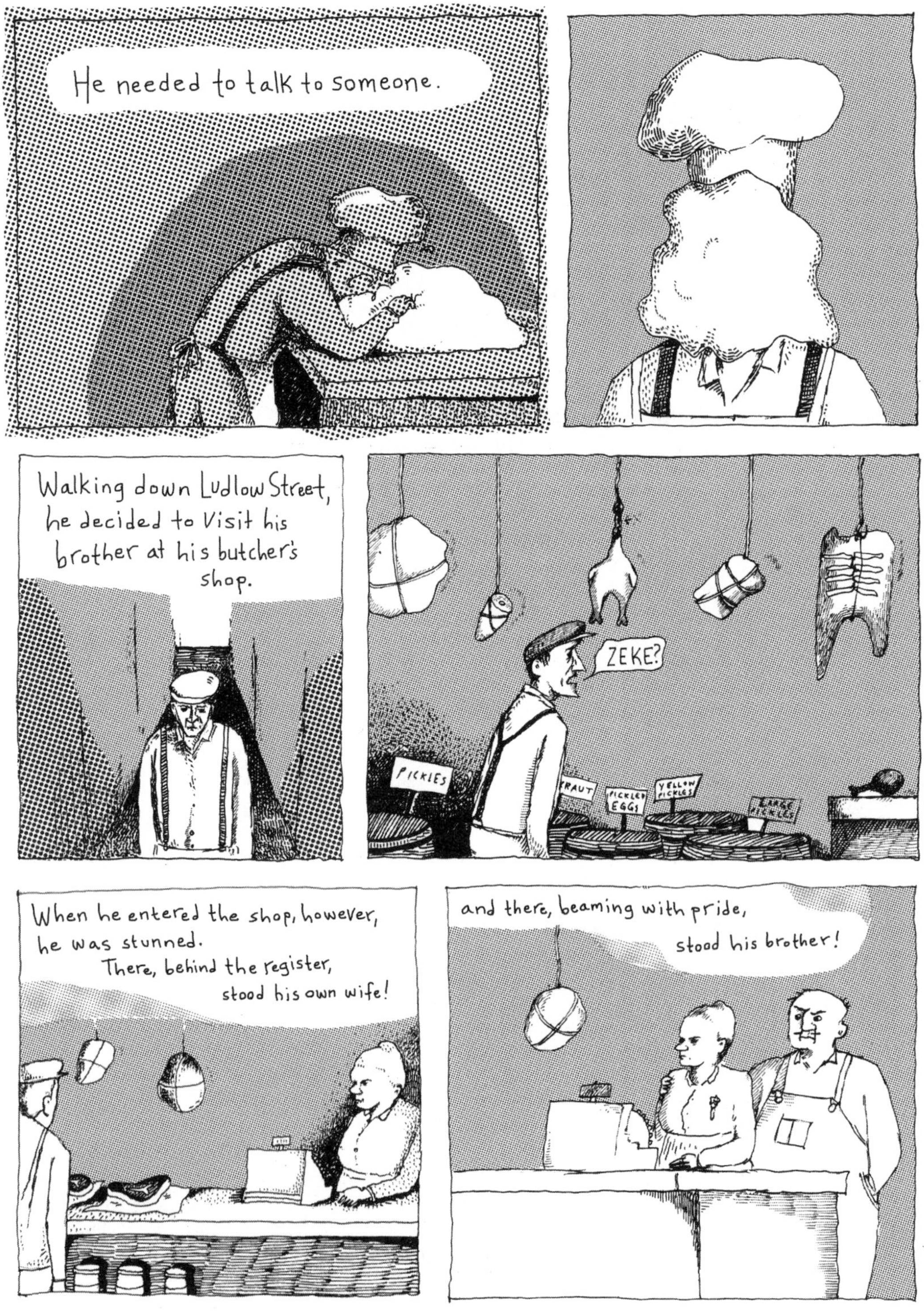
He needed to talk to someone.
Walking down Ludlow Street, he decided to visit his brother at his butcher's shop.
ZEKE?
PICKLES
KRAUT
PICKLED EGGS
YELLOW PICKLES
LARGE PICKLES
When he entered the shop, however, he was stunned. There, behind the register, stood his own wife!
and there, beaming with pride, stood his brother!

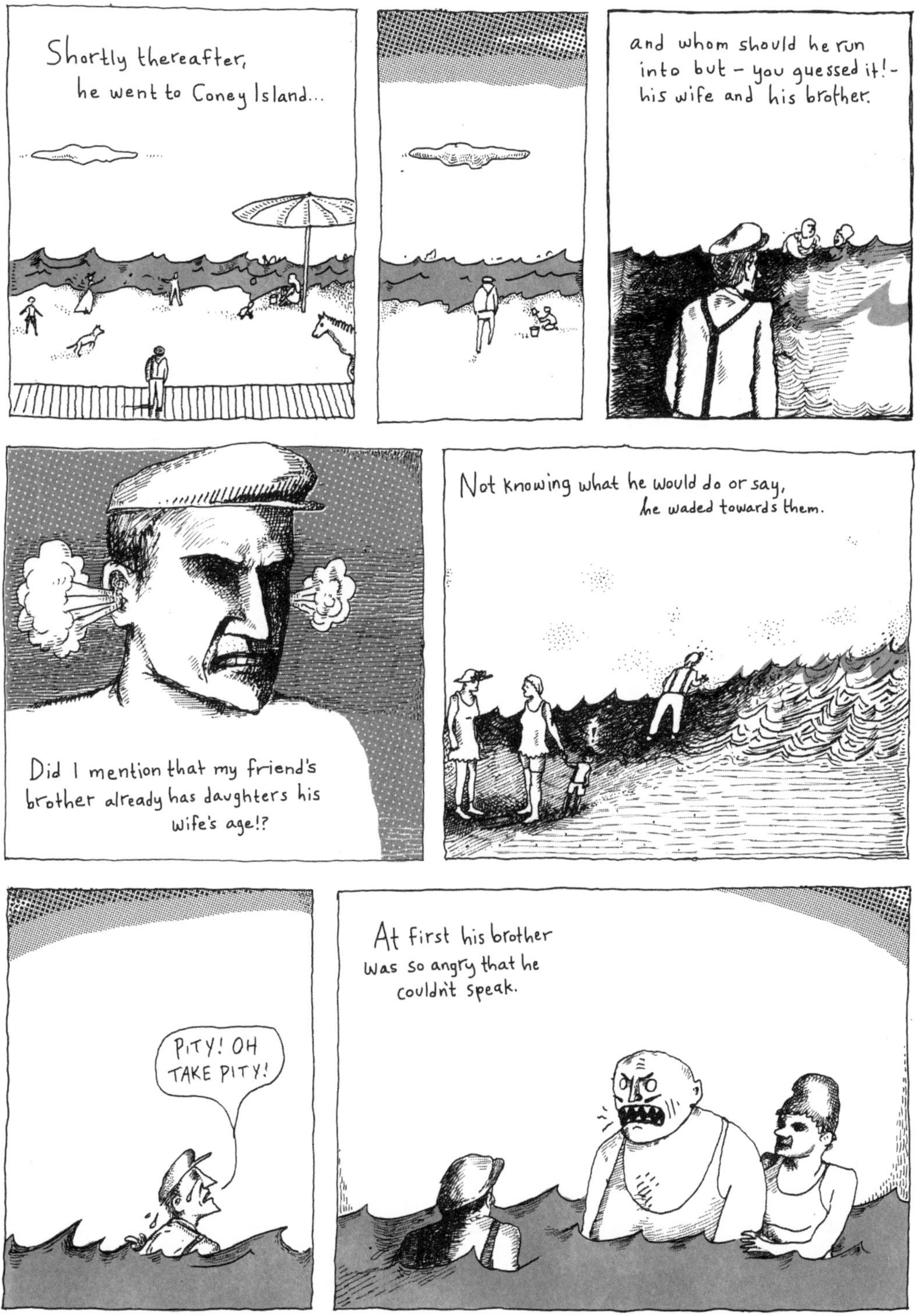
Shortly thereafter, he went to Coney Island...
and whom should he run into but - you guessed it! - his wife and his brother.
Did I mention that my friend's brother already has daughters his wife's age!?
Not knowing what he would do or say, he waded towards them.
PITY! OH TAKE PITY!
At first his brother was so angry that he couldn't speak.

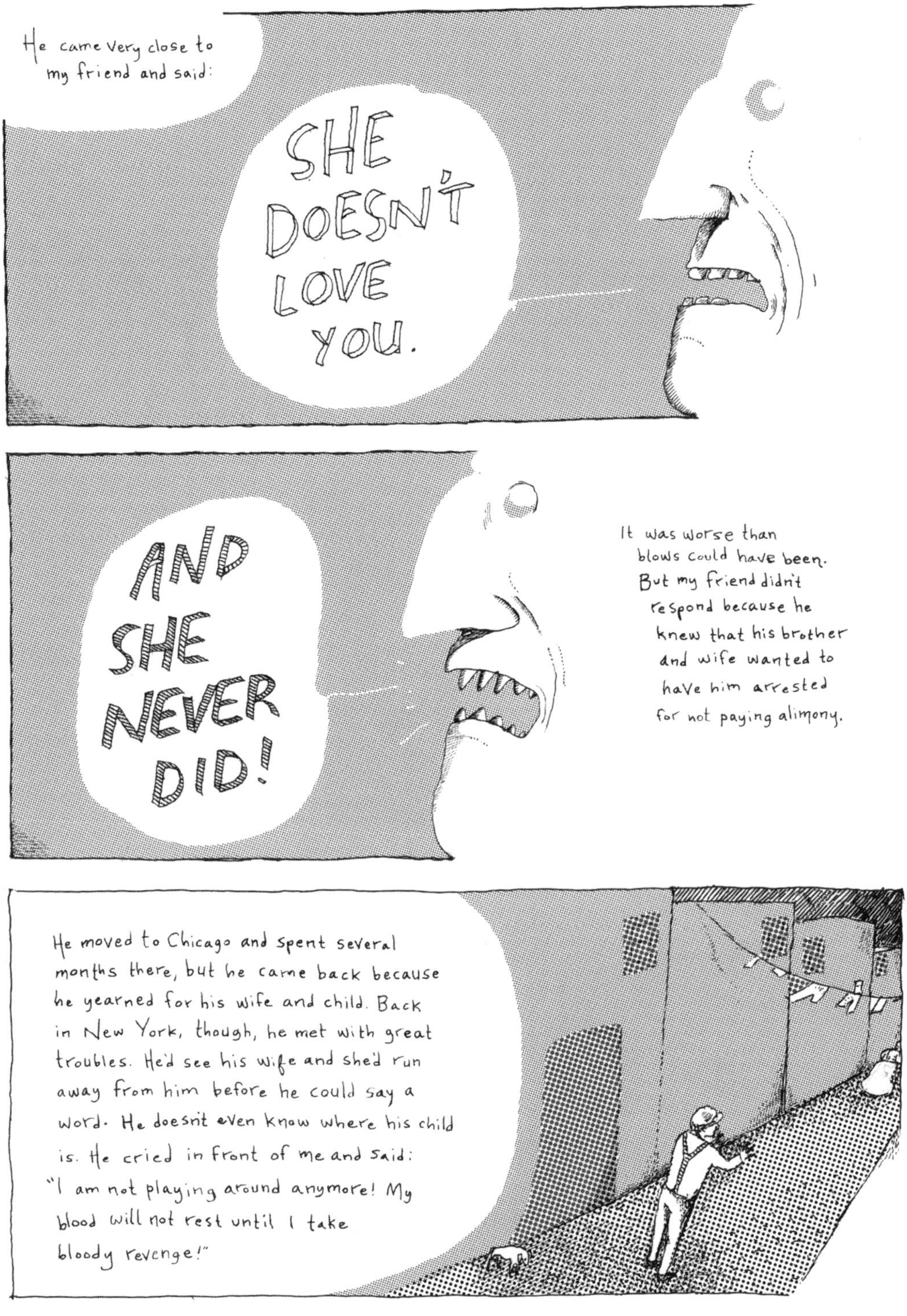
He came very close to my friend and said:
SHE DOESN'T LOVE YOU.
AND SHE NEVER DID!
It was worse than blows could have been. But my friend didn't respond because he knew that his brother and wife wanted to have him arrested for not paying alimony.
He moved to Chicago and spent several months there, but he came back because he yearned for his wife and child. Back in New York, though, he met with great troubles. He'd see his wife and she'd run away from him before he could say a word. He doesn't even know where his child is. He cried in front of me and said: "I am not playing around anymore! My blood will not rest until I take bloody revenge!"

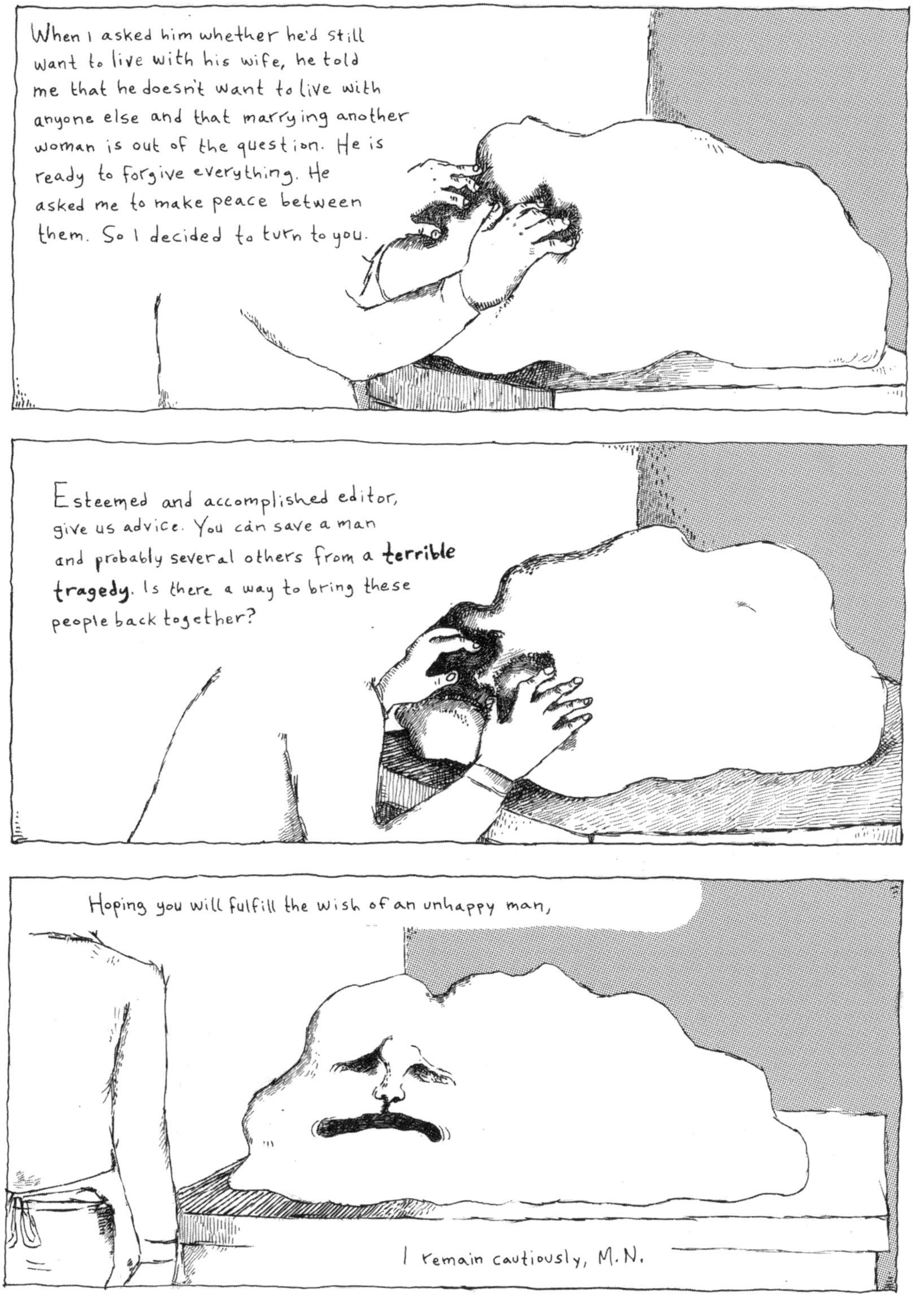
When I asked him whether he'd still want to live with his wife, he told me that he doesn't want to live with anyone else and that marrying another woman is out of the question. He is ready to forgive everything. He asked me to make peace between them. So I decided to turn to you.
Esteemed and accomplished editor, give us advice. You can save a man and probably several others from a **terrible tragedy**. Is there a way to bring these people back together?
Hoping you will fulfill the wish of an unhappy man,
I remain cautiously, M.N.

Considering how the woman is described here (if no important facts, explanations or details are missing), we don't see anyone to make peace with. For the writer's countryman the best option is to try to calm down. Right now he thinks that he'll never be able to live without her. This is only what he thinks. If her current actions are only the result of inexperience and frivolousness she will one day take great pity on him.

With Cahan too preoccupied by the "modern world" to answer my questions, I decided to take my education into my own hands.

In the main branch of the New York Public Library, I found early issues of **The Forward** preserved on microfilm.

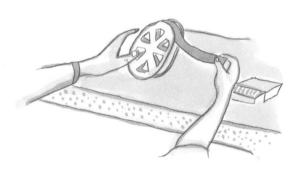

I couldn't read the articles because they were in Yiddish, but the photographs in the paper haunted me. There was a series of portraits of men's faces that made me particularly sad and lonely. I didn't know why, but I couldn't look away.

I found out later that the pictures were of men who had abandoned their families or disappeared. So many women were writing to the Bintel Brief with pictures of their delinquent husbands and notes pleading with them to come home, that "A Gallery of Missing Husbands" spun off and became its own newspaper feature.

THE GALLERY of MISSING HUSBANDS

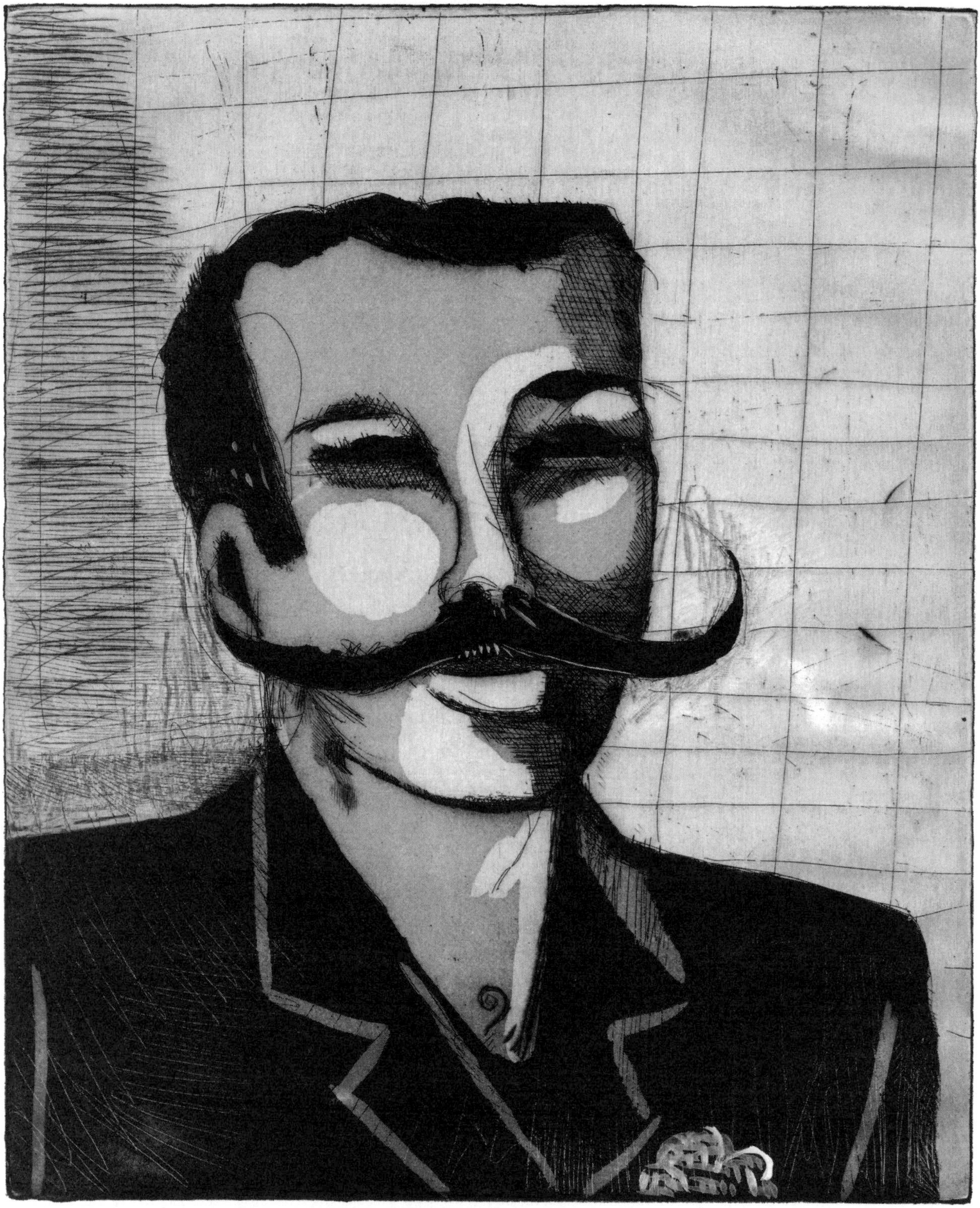

CHAYIM, 35

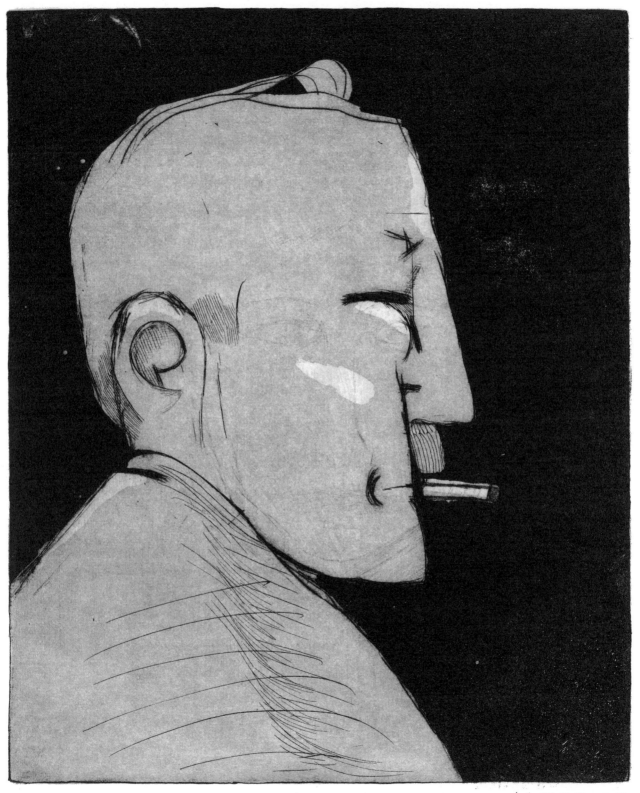

ALTER,42

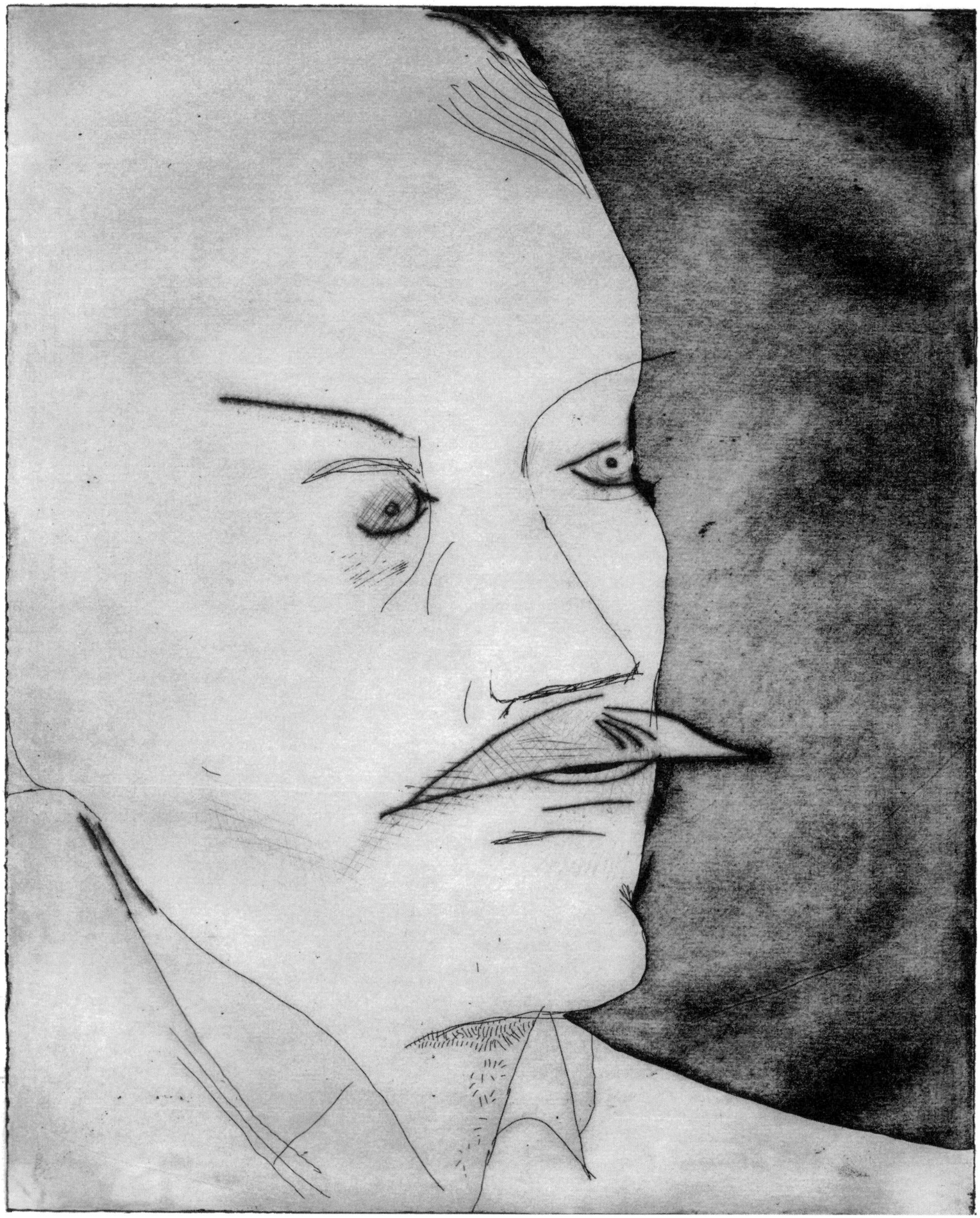

MENDEL, 38

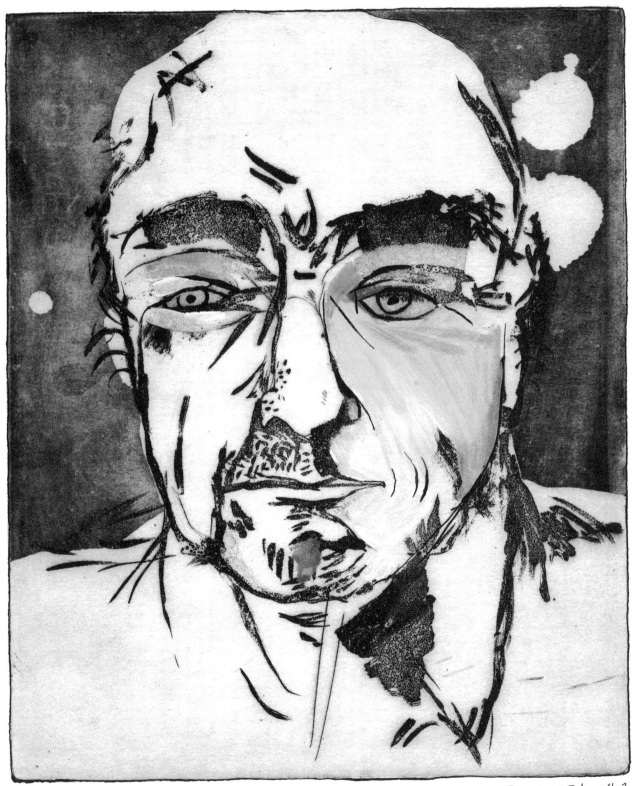

SHMUEL, 41

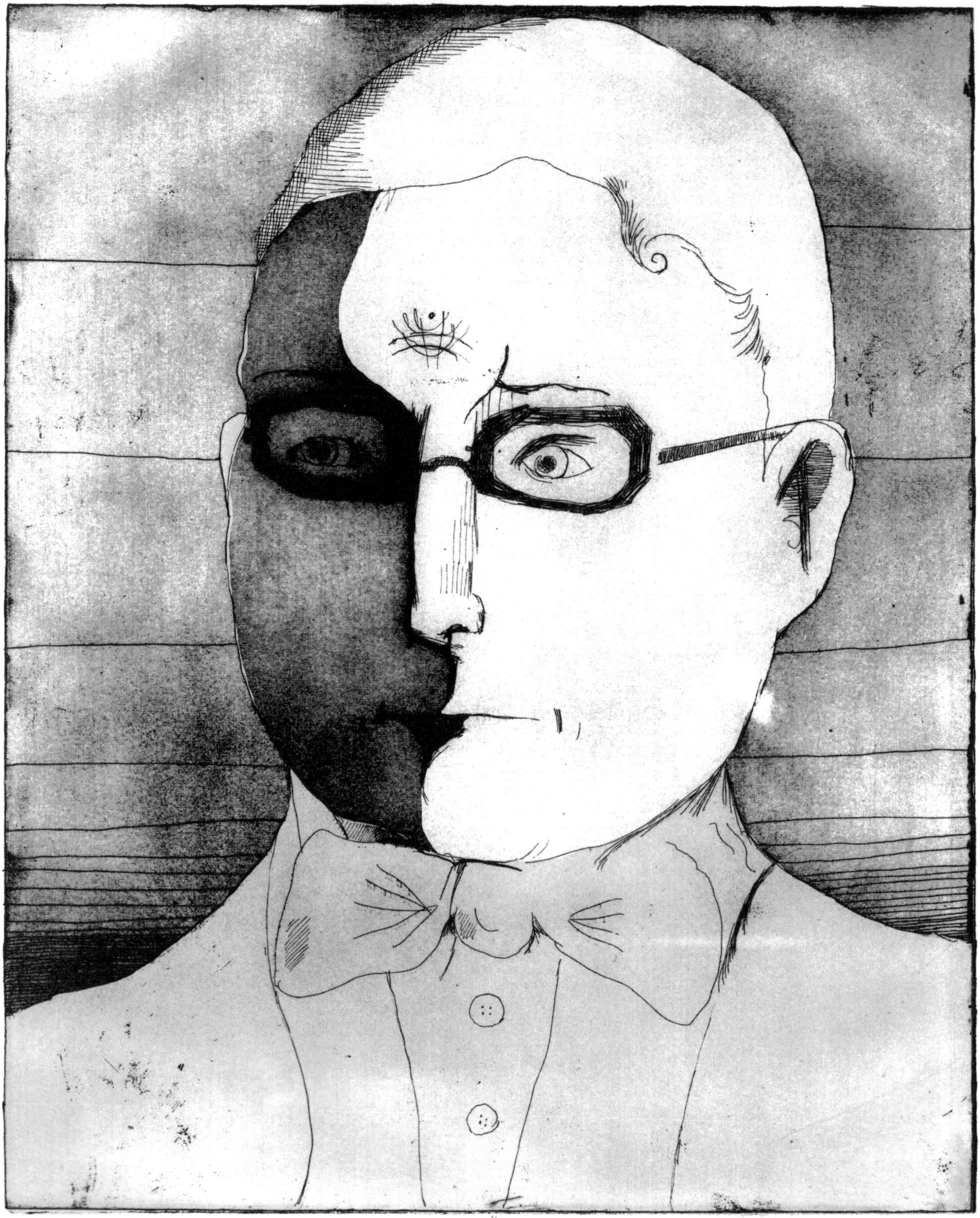

FISHKE, 25

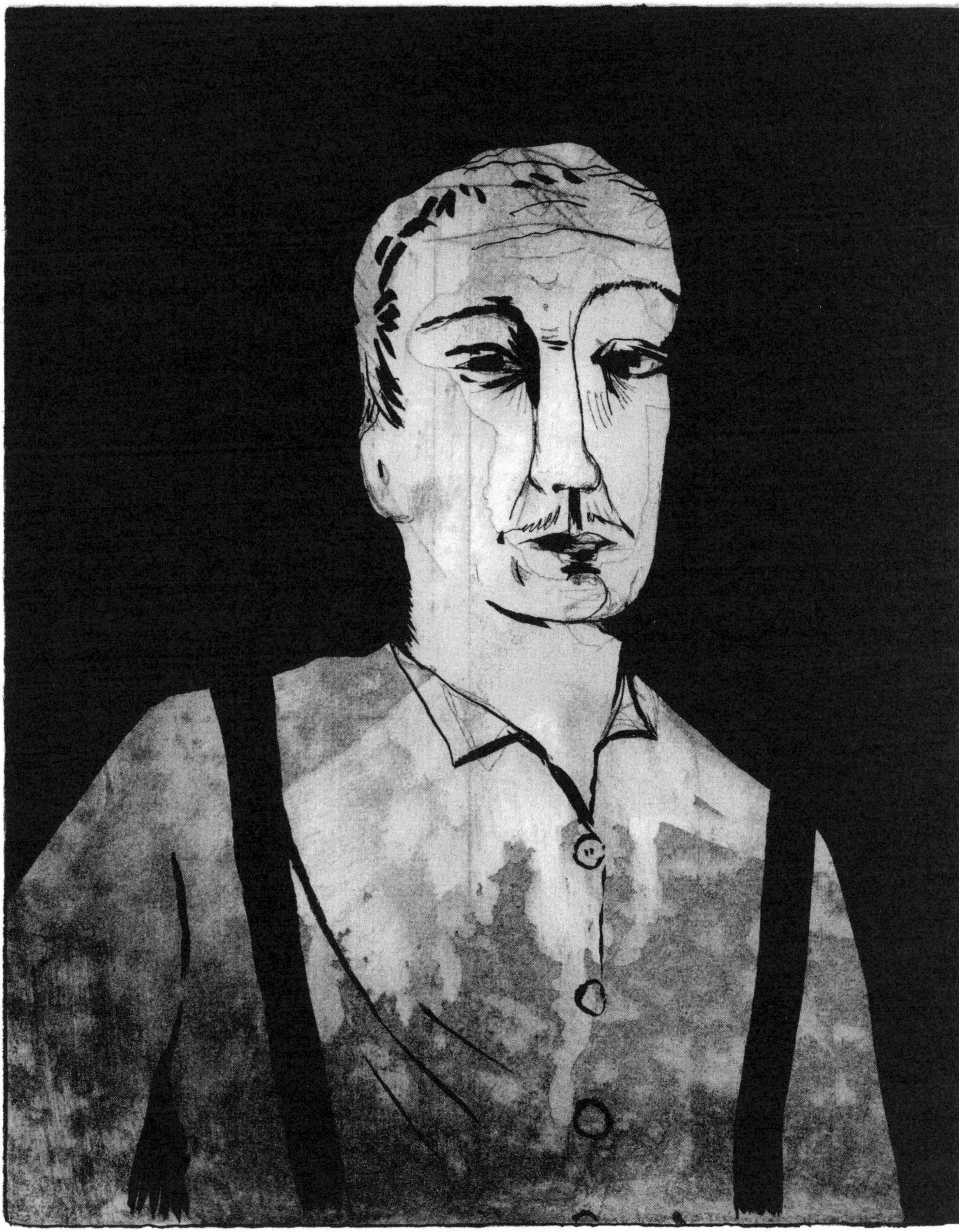

MOSHE, 29

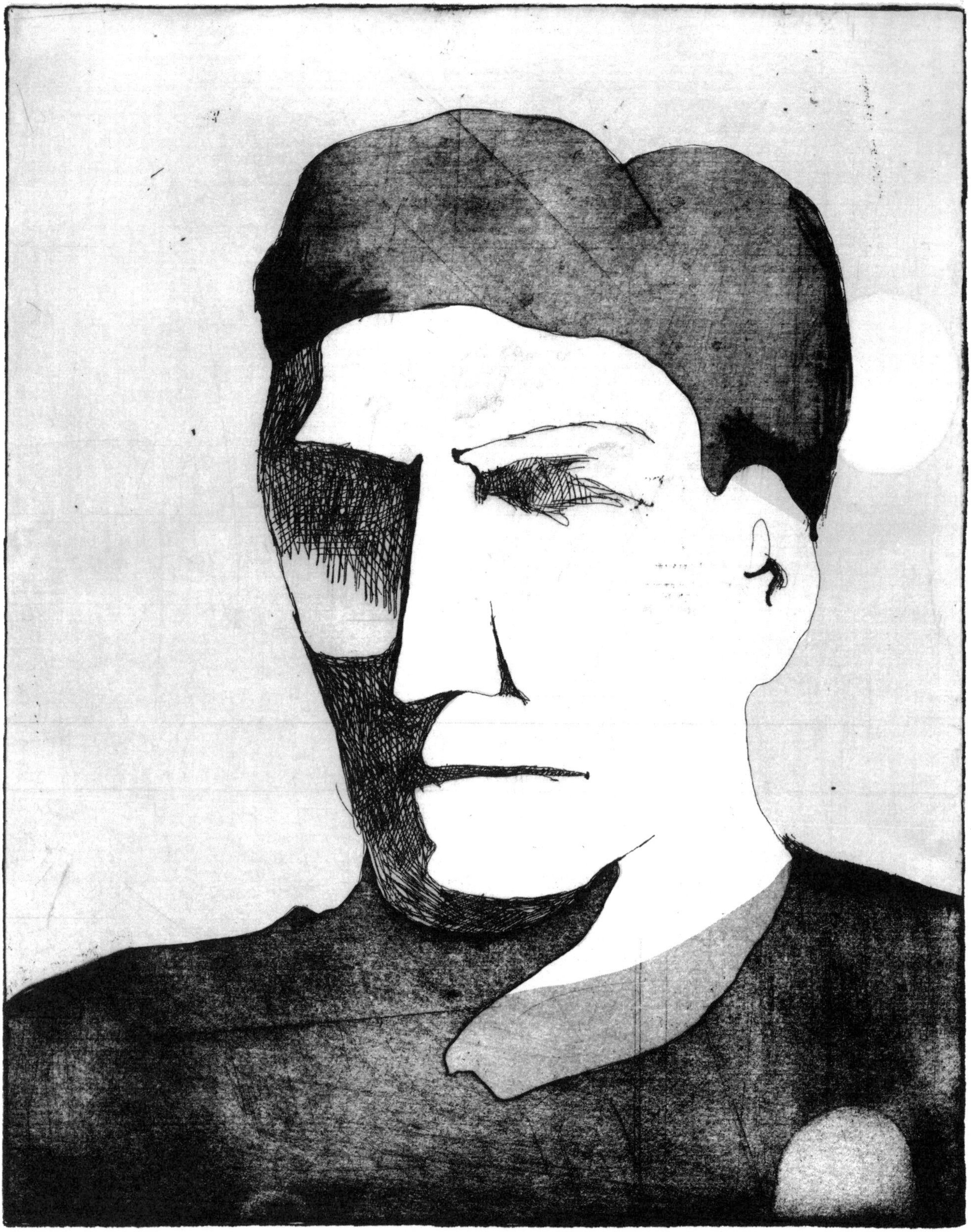

SAUL, 24

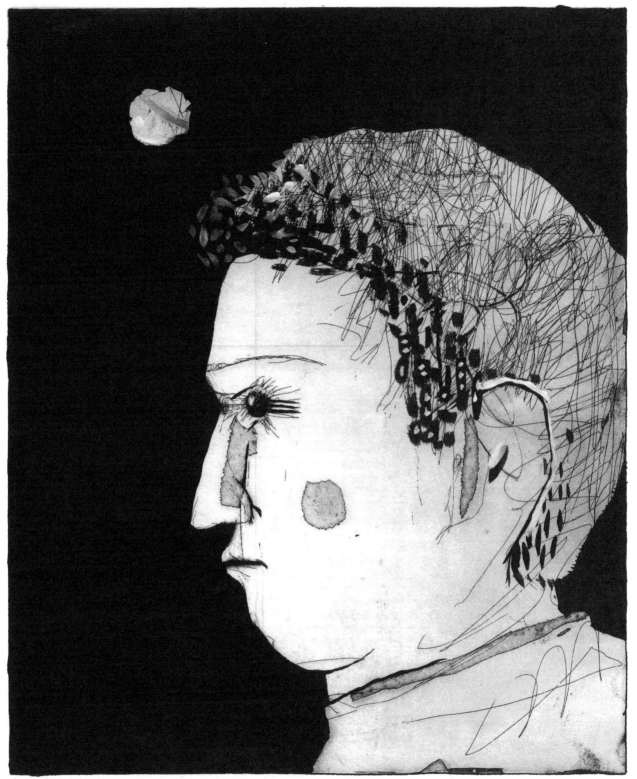

ISAAC, 23

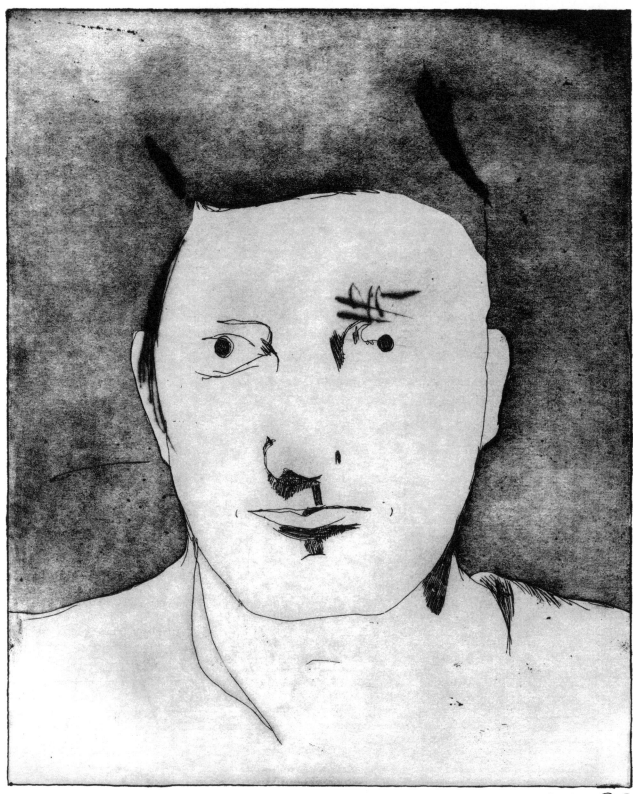

MAX, 28

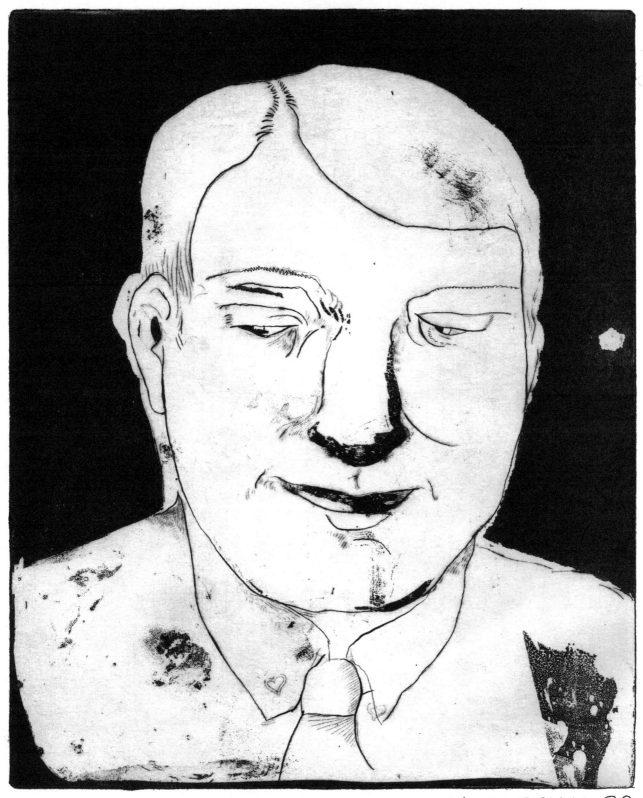

MORDECHAI, 30

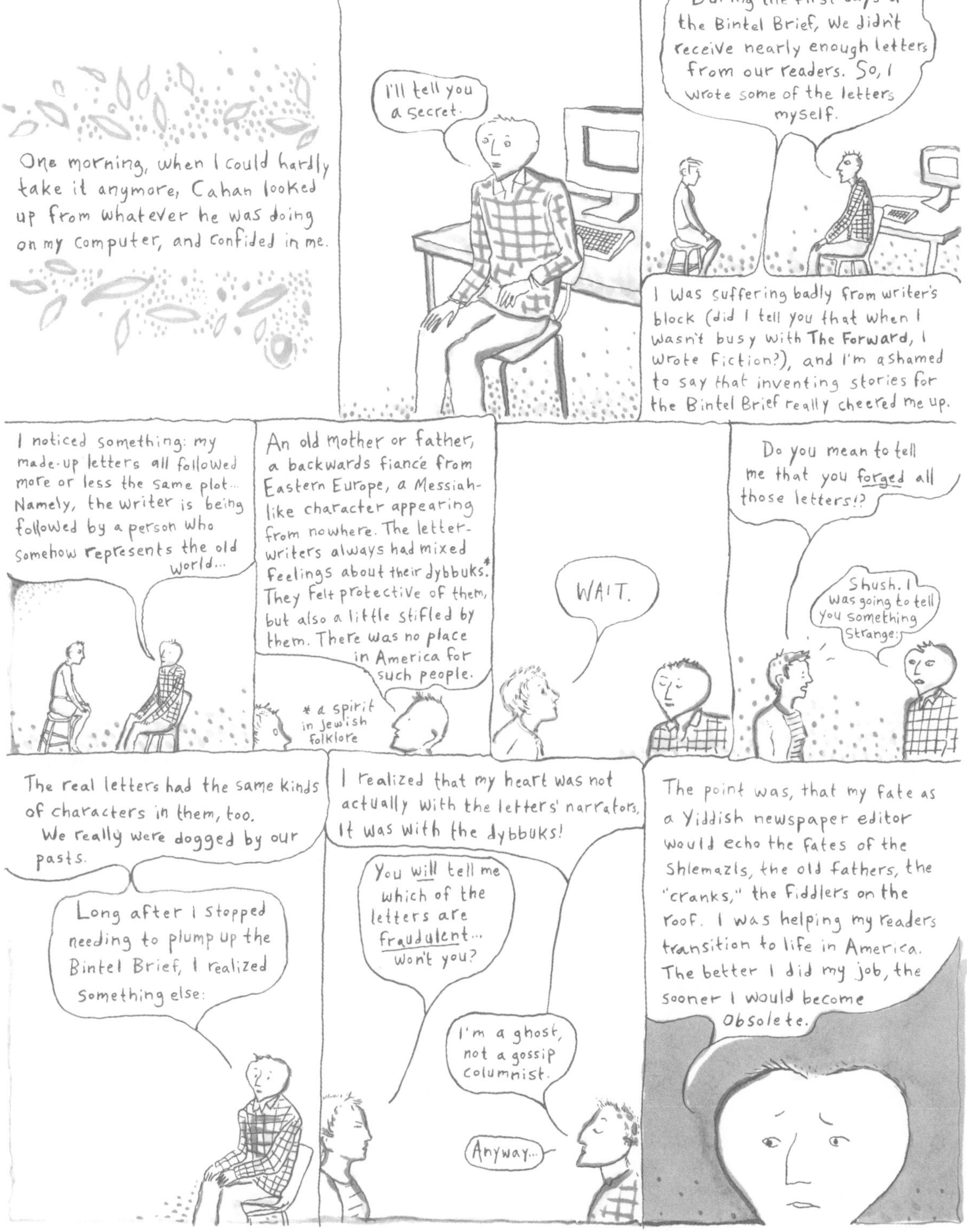
One morning, when I could hardly take it anymore, Cahan looked up from whatever he was doing on my computer, and confided in me.
I'll tell you a secret.
During the first days of the Bintel Brief, we didn't receive nearly enough letters from our readers. So, I wrote some of the letters myself.
I was suffering badly from writer's block (did I tell you that when I wasn't busy with The Forward, I wrote fiction?), and I'm ashamed to say that inventing stories for the Bintel Brief really cheered me up.
I noticed something: my made-up letters all followed more or less the same plot... Namely, the writer is being followed by a person who somehow represents the old world...
An old mother or father, a backwards fiancé from Eastern Europe, a Messiah-like character appearing from nowhere. The letter-writers always had mixed feelings about their dybbuks.* They felt protective of them, but also a little stifled by them. There was no place in America for such people.
* a spirit in Jewish folklore
WAIT.
Do you mean to tell me that you forged all those letters!?
Shush. I was going to tell you something strange:
The real letters had the same kinds of characters in them, too. We really were dogged by our pasts.
Long after I stopped needing to plump up the Bintel Brief, I realized something else:
I realized that my heart was not actually with the letters' narrators, It was with the dybbuks!
You will tell me which of the letters are fraudulent... won't you?
I'm a ghost, not a gossip columnist.
Anyway...
The point was, that my fate as a Yiddish newspaper editor would echo the fates of the shlemazls, the old fathers, the "cranks," the Fiddlers on the roof. I was helping my readers transition to life in America. The better I did my job, the sooner I would become obsolete.

9

A CRIMINAL

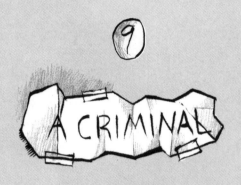

Honored **Forward** Editor,

I'm a woman. I married my first husband nine years ago. I married without the knowledge of my mother and against her will. And I paid greatly for my mother's pain, for my marriage was a bed of suffering. Finally, I rallied my strength and fled. I came to America. Here, people think of me as a proper young lady. And I do not set them straight because I could not bear to be surrounded by people who know the truth about me.

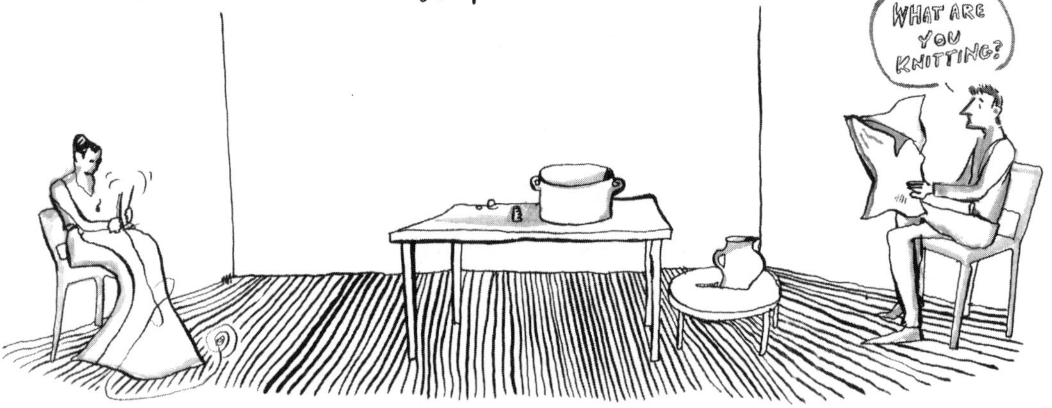
WHAT ARE YOU KNITTING?

I was sure that I'd never love again. But time changes everything. Two years ago, I met a consumptive young man. Truth be told, I understood very little of his character the first year I knew him. But as time went on I got to know him better and became acquainted with his kindness and his noble ideals.

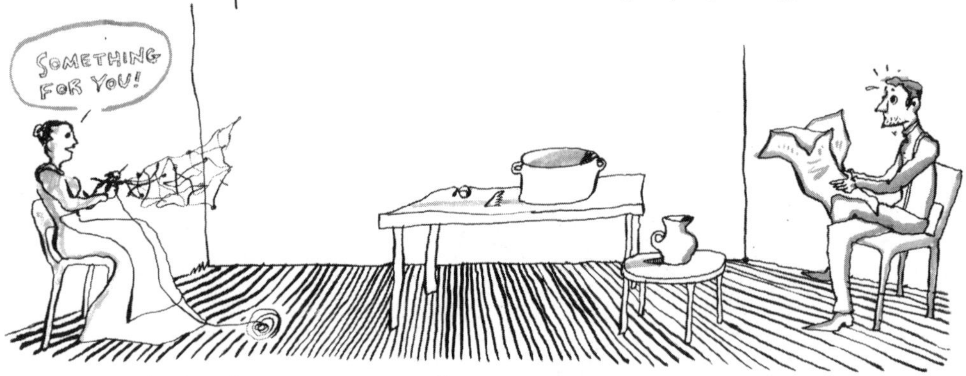
SOMETHING FOR YOU!

Short and sweet: I've been married to this man for several months. Oh, how sad it is to love someone who is ill! All of my friends called me a criminal for marrying such a man, for whom the strain of married life could be severely dangerous. But I knew of several cases in which consumptives were actually cured by marriage, and on these miracles I fixed my sights.

If only I had investigated my soul more closely. Then I would have protected the health of a twenty-five-year-old man who was noble, good, honest and full of hope. And with my meanness and my broken character, I killed him.

IT'S NOT GOING TO BE A WEB, IS IT?

As soon as I became his wife I went back to my old habits. I am very nervous and have a violent temper. When I get angry I go into a trance and attack the weakest parts of the people I love. I am eating out my husband's poor heart. So far, I have only used words, but it is just a matter of time before I become physically violent.

NO! DON'T WORRY. I'VE CHANGED MY WAYS.

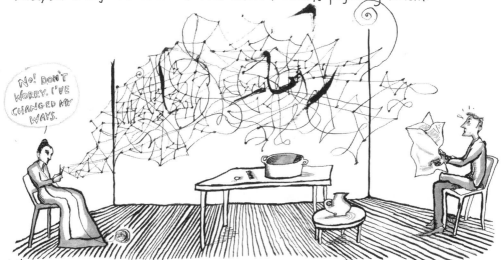

When I wake up in the morning I am remorseful. I vow to be good to him. But some little thing always sets me off and I become my old self in a minute. What should I do? A known murderer is at least punished, but I am an unknown murderer.

I would sentence myself and take my own life, but part of me still believes I'll change my ways. Besides, the life I lead now is worse than death. I didn't know until now that a murderer also has a conscience. Mine doesn't permit me to rest. I've ruined my husband's life. Before we met, he had a nice home and many friends. But I spent recklessly so that we had to give up the house, and his friends hate me. My husband has never been so sick as he's been these past few months, and because of me he's been forced to work in a sweatshop. He won't accept help from anyone because he's very proud, and I've had to work as a servant. My situation is awful, but I don't complain. This is far too small of a punishment for me.

Esteemed editor! I request your advice. Can I fix what I have destroyed? My situation is not that bad but my husband's *is* deplorable. I am greatly uncertain and wait for your counsel.

    signed,

    The Spider

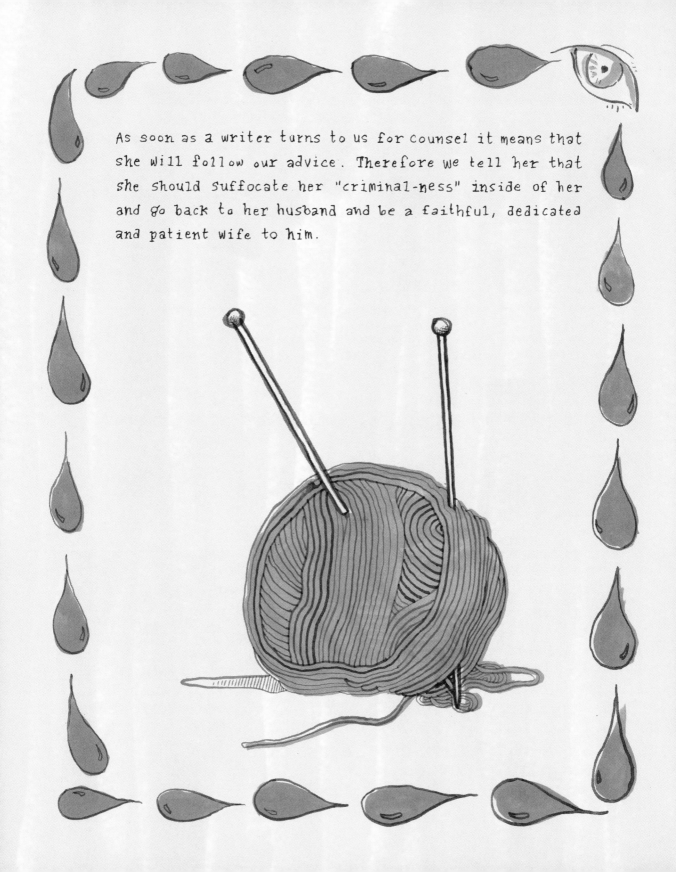

As soon as a writer turns to us for counsel it means that she will follow our advice. Therefore we tell her that she should suffocate her "criminal-ness" inside of her and go back to her husband and be a faithful, dedicated and patient wife to him.

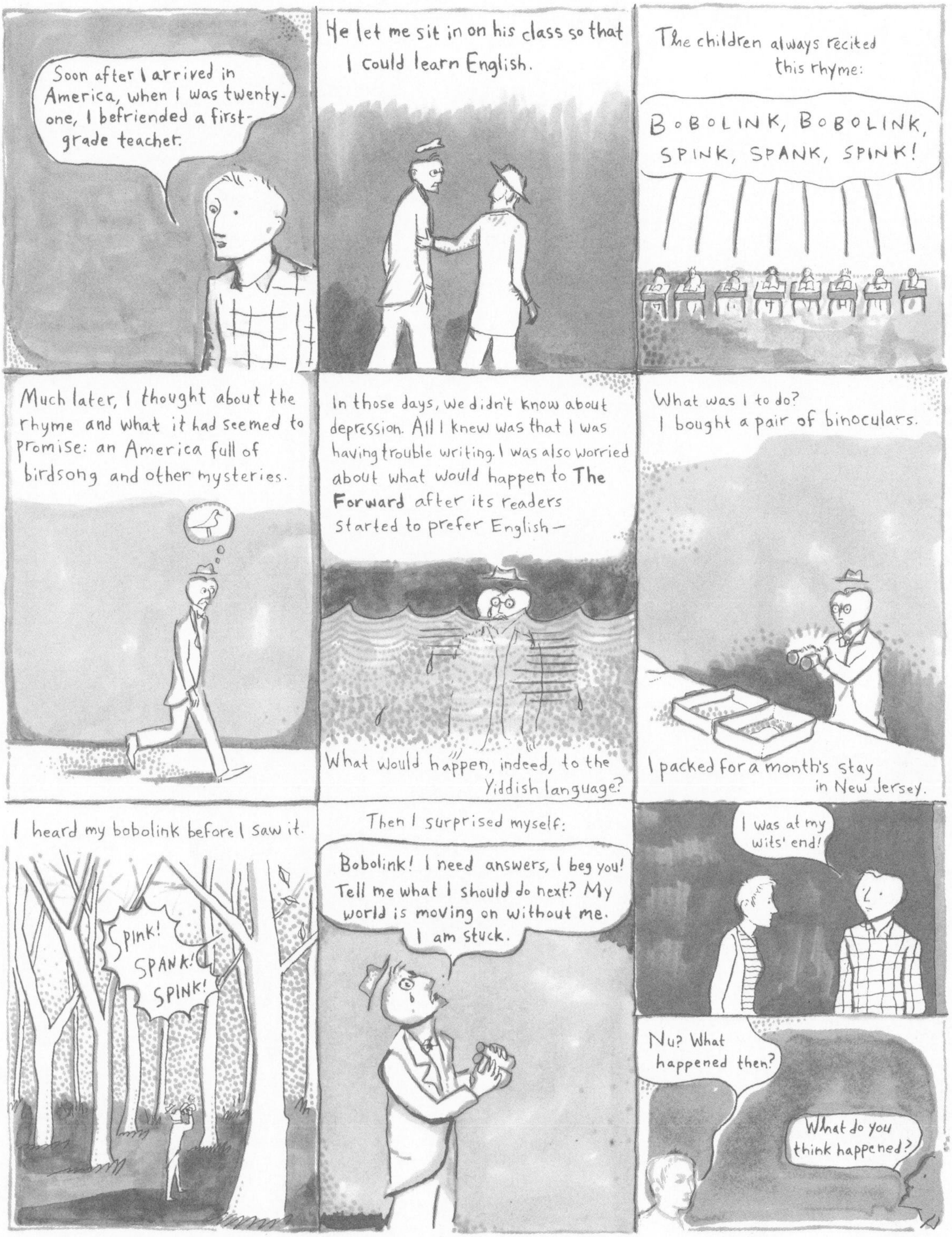

Soon after I arrived in America, when I was twenty-one, I befriended a first-grade teacher.
He let me sit in on his class so that I could learn English.
The children always recited this rhyme:
BOBOLINK, BOBOLINK, SPINK, SPANK, SPINK!
Much later, I thought about the rhyme and what it had seemed to promise: an America full of birdsong and other mysteries.
In those days, we didn't know about depression. All I knew was that I was having trouble writing. I was also worried about what would happen to **The Forward** after its readers started to prefer English—
What would happen, indeed, to the Yiddish language?
What was I to do? I bought a pair of binoculars.
I packed for a month's stay in New Jersey.
I heard my bobolink before I saw it.
SPINK! SPANK! SPINK!
Then I surprised myself:
Bobolink! I need answers, I beg you! Tell me what I should do next? My world is moving on without me. I am stuck.
I was at my wits' end!
Nu? What happened then?
What do you think happened?

THE MELANCHOLY
CANTOR

Dear Mr. Editor,

I come from Europe, where my father was a Talmud scholar and a cantor.

I took after my father, both in learning—

And in voice—

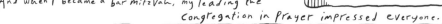

And when I became a bar mitzvah, my leading the congregation in prayer impressed everyone.

My name became known in many cities, and people came from far and wide to hear me conduct the services.

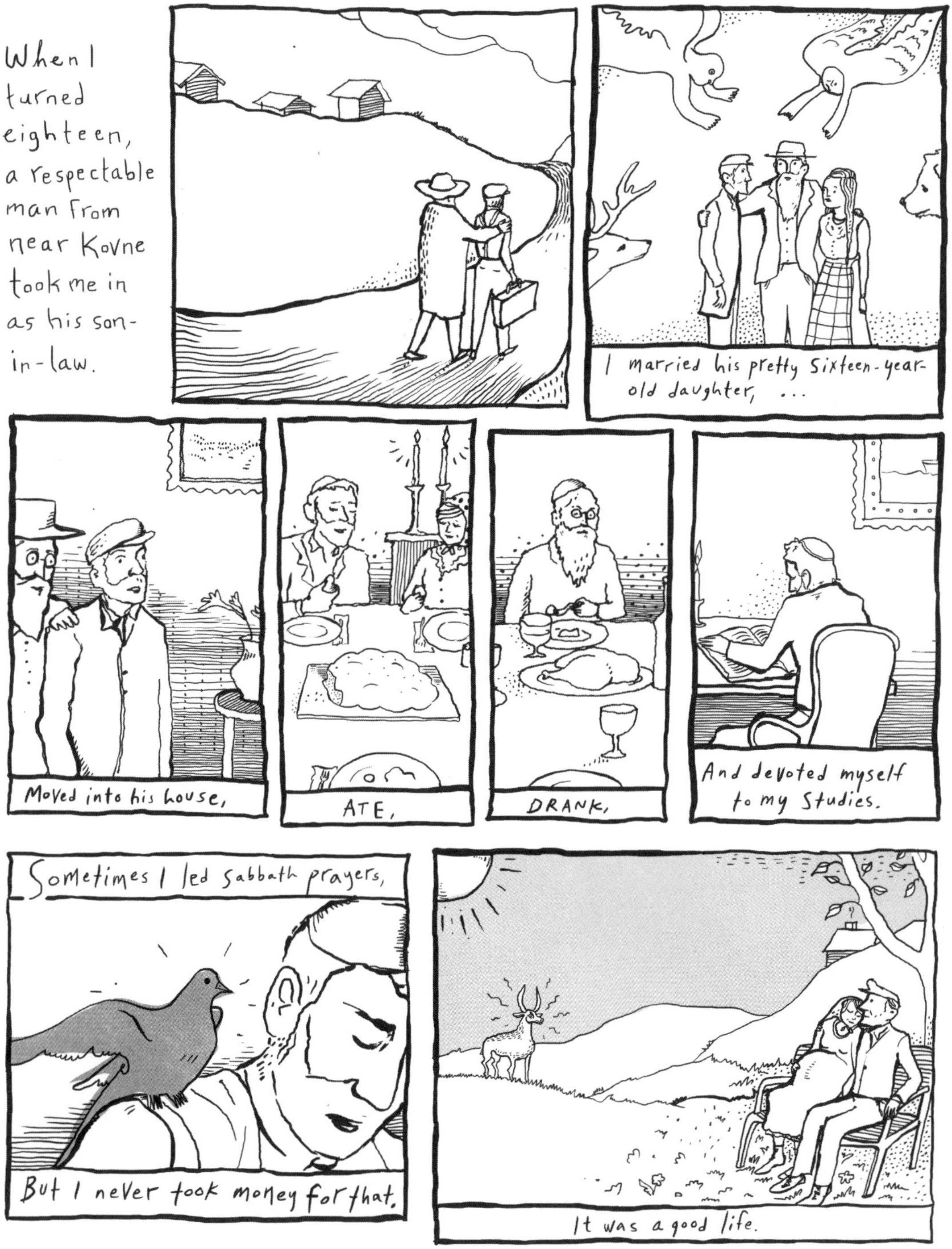
When I turned eighteen, a respectable man from near Kovne took me in as his son-in-law.
I married his pretty sixteen-year-old daughter, ...
Moved into his house,
ATE,
DRANK,
And devoted myself to my studies.
Sometimes I led sabbath prayers,
But I never took money for that.
It was a good life.

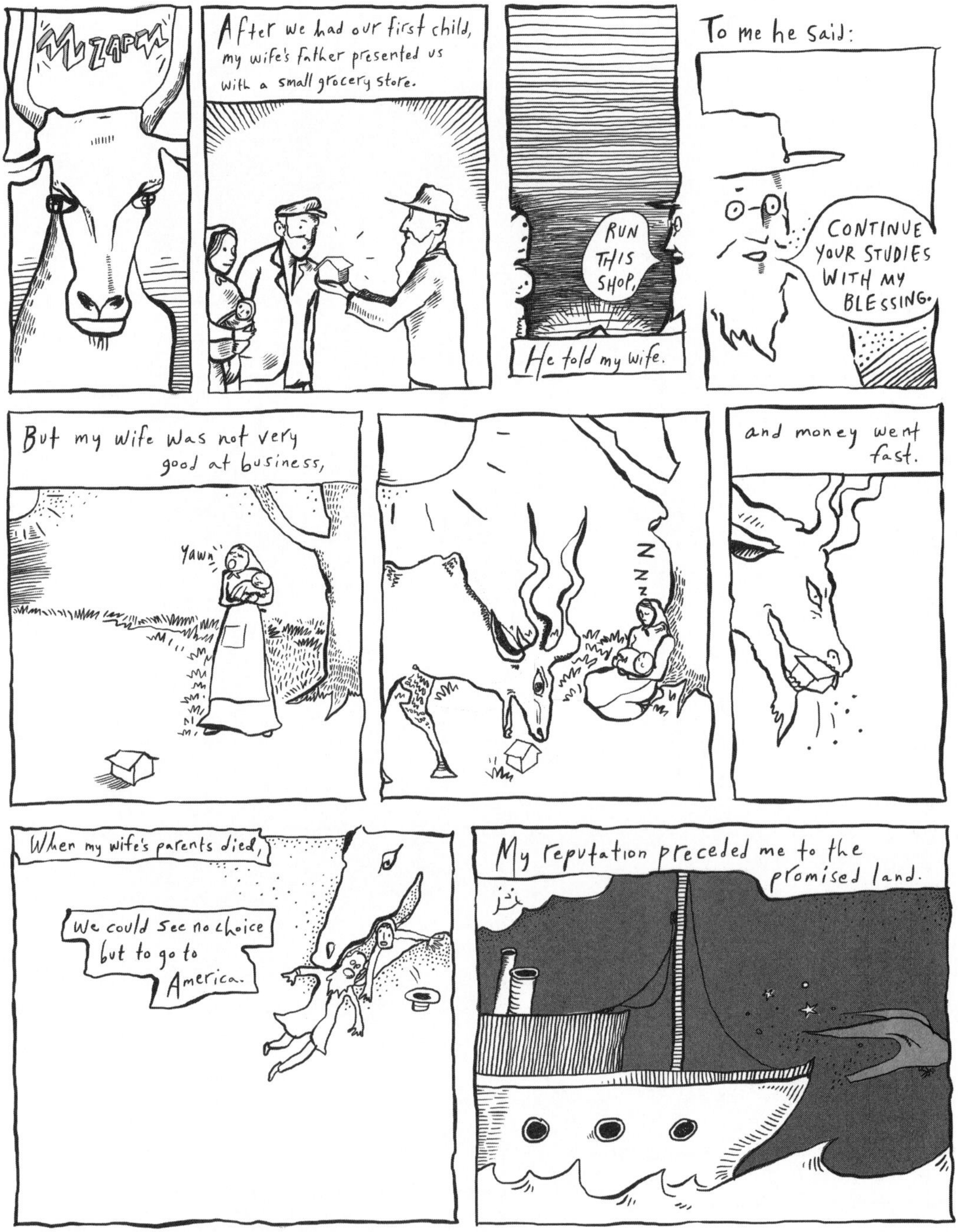

ZZAPM
After we had our first child, my wife's father presented us with a small grocery store.
RUN THIS SHOP,
He told my wife.
To me he said:
CONTINUE YOUR STUDIES WITH MY BLESSING.
But my wife was not very good at business,
YAWN
Z Z Z
and money went fast.
When my wife's parents died,
we could see no choice but to go to America.
My reputation preceded me to the promised land.

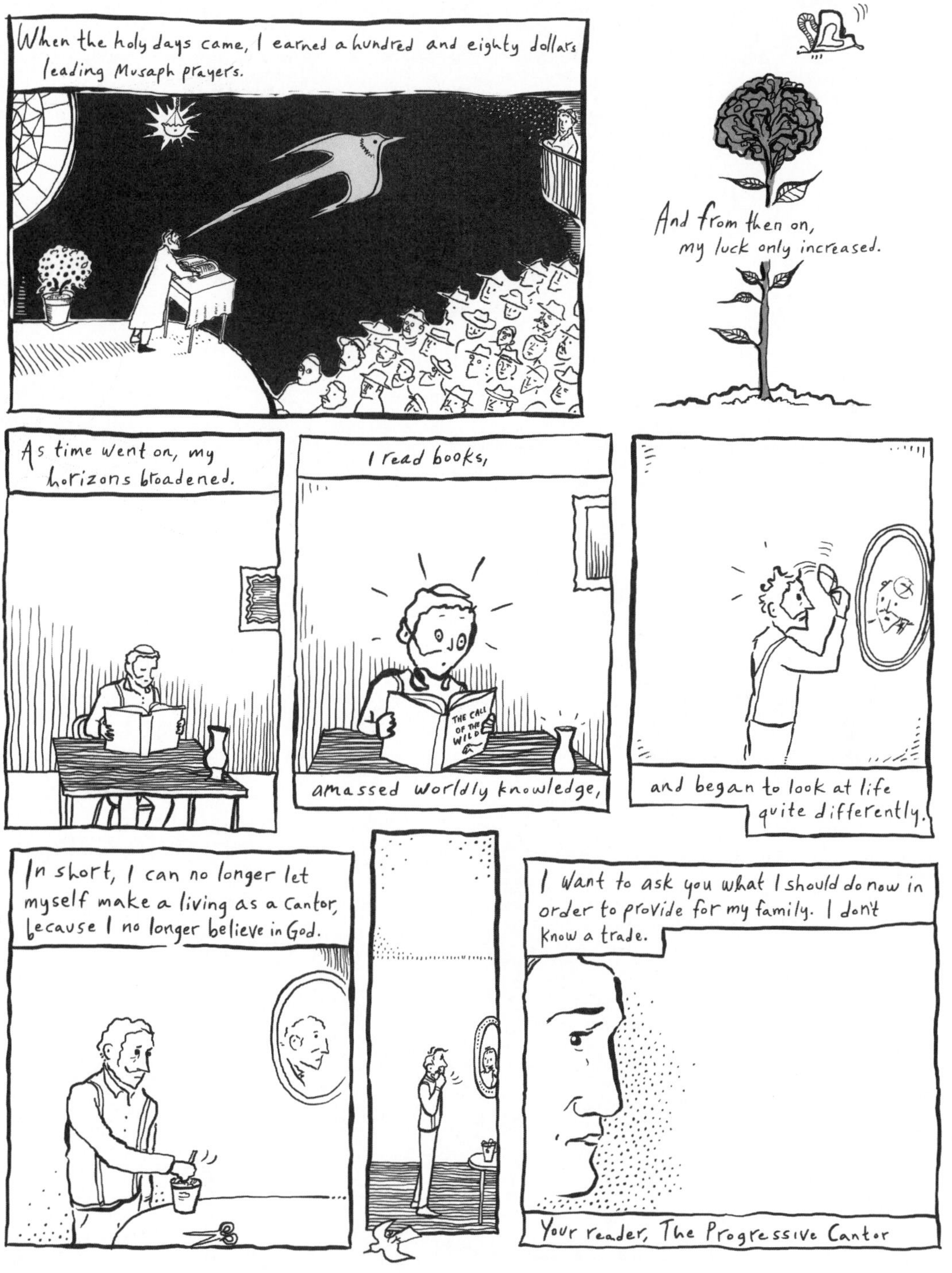
When the holy days came, I earned a hundred and eighty dollars leading Musaph prayers.
And from then on, my luck only increased.
As time went on, my horizons broadened.
I read books,
THE CALL OF THE WILD
amassed worldly knowledge,
and began to look at life quite differently.
In short, I can no longer let myself make a living as a Cantor, because I no longer believe in God.
I want to ask you what I should do now in order to provide for my family. I don't know a trade.
Your reader, The Progressive Cantor

Freethinkers as well as religious people will answer this question in the same way. Even the rabbi will say that, according to Jewish law, only a pious Jew may be a cantor. His wife and his religious friends who are trying to convince him to remain a cantor are really committing the worst sin according to their beliefs.

For a nonbeliever to be a cantor for an orthodox congregation is without a doubt a shameful hypocrisy.

We know of several talented singers who, when they stopped believing, found work singing in the theater. There may be other opportunities for you to make use of and honor your voice.

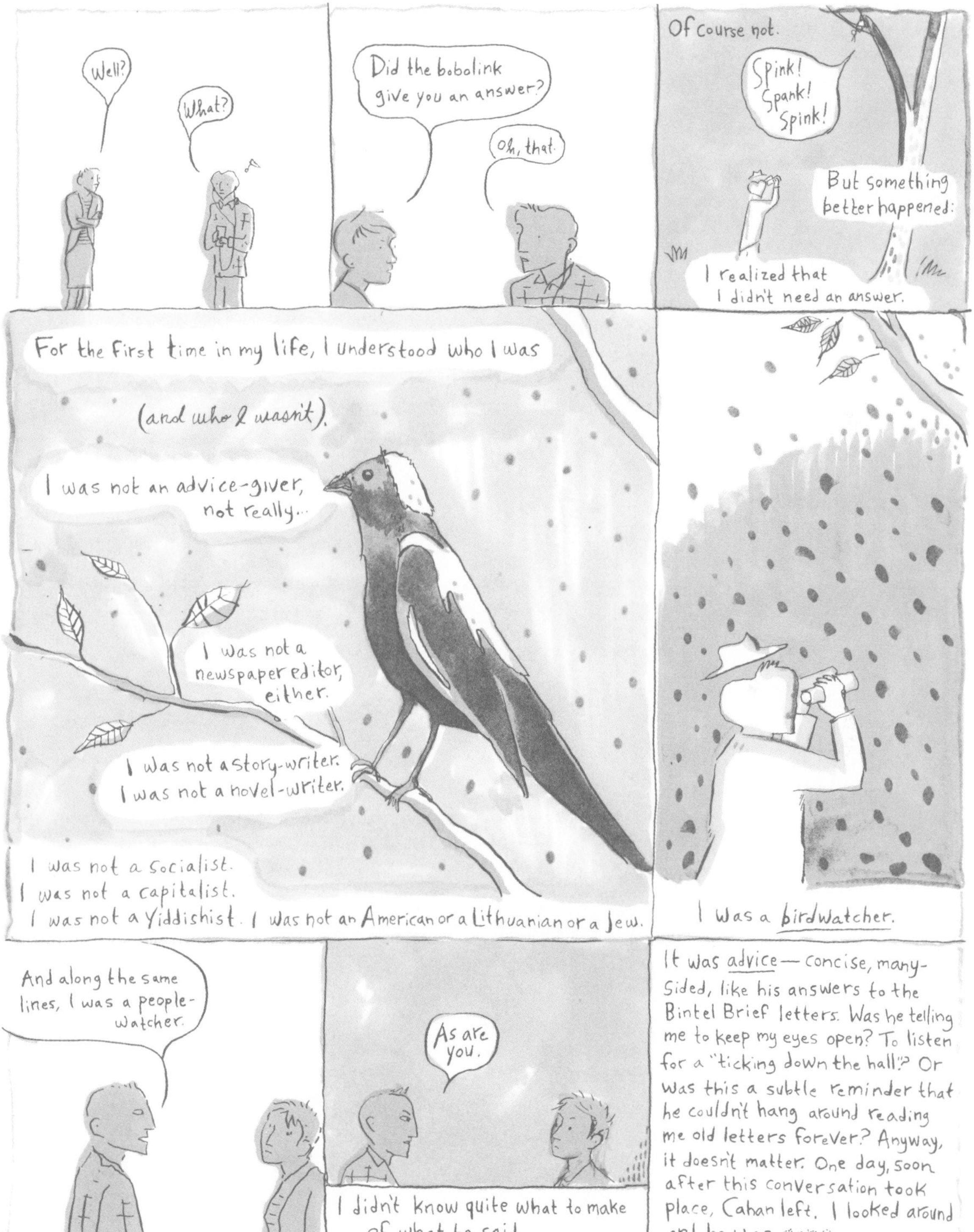
Well?
What?
Did the bobolink give you an answer?
Oh, that.
Of course not.
Spink! Spank! Spink!
But something better happened:
I realized that I didn't need an answer.
For the first time in my life, I understood who I was
(and who I wasn't).
I was not an advice-giver, not really...
I was not a newspaper editor, either.
I was not a story-writer. I was not a novel-writer.
I was not a socialist.
I was not a capitalist.
I was not a Yiddishist. I was not an American or a Lithuanian or a Jew.
I was a birdwatcher.
And along the same lines, I was a people-watcher.
As are you.
I didn't know quite what to make of what he said.
It was advice — concise, many-sided, like his answers to the Bintel Brief letters. Was he telling me to keep my eyes open? To listen for a "ticking down the hall"? Or was this a subtle reminder that he couldn't hang around reading me old letters forever? Anyway, it doesn't matter. One day, soon after this conversation took place, Cahan left. I looked around and he was gone.

11

A FAITHFUL READER

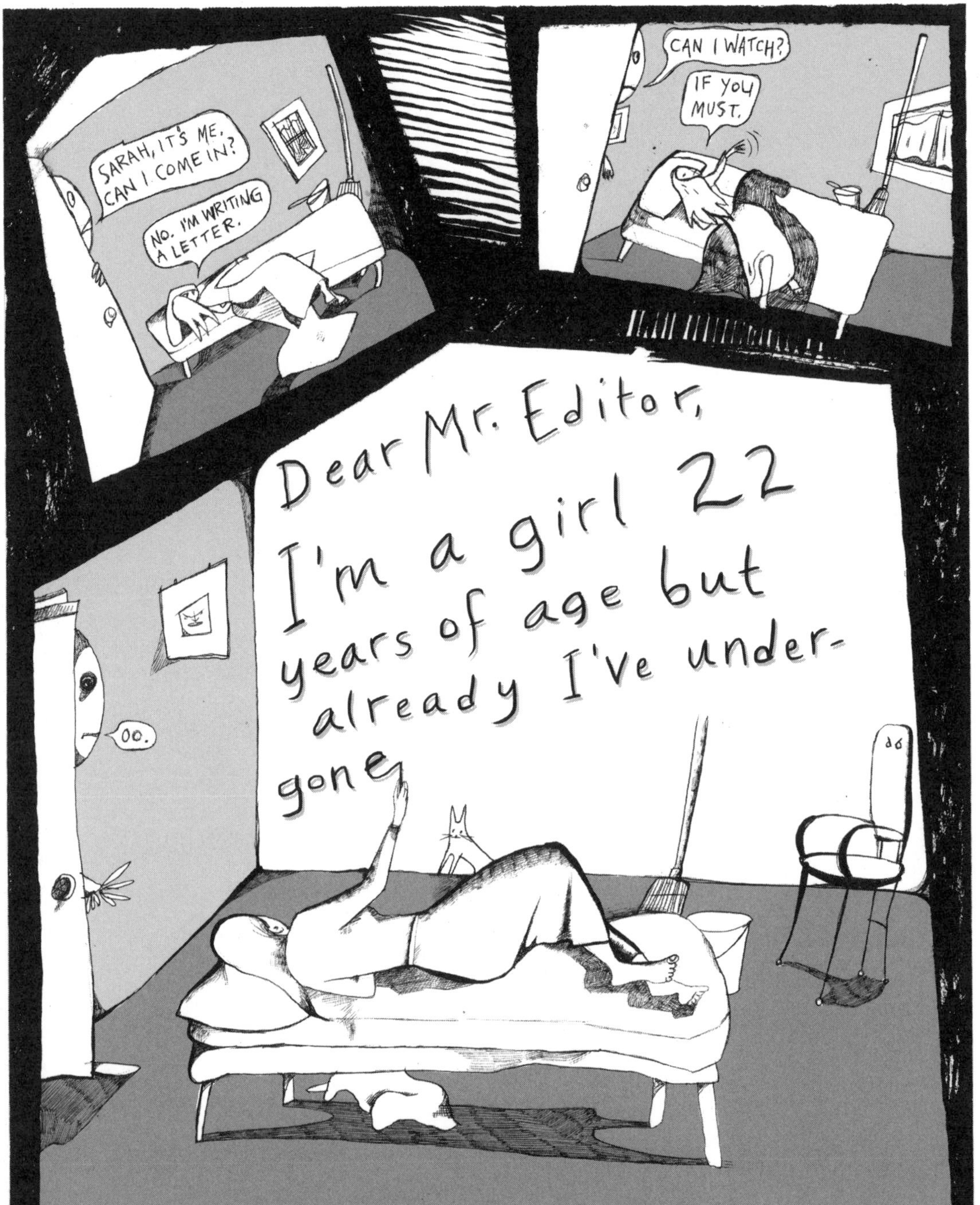
SARAH, IT'S ME. CAN I COME IN?
NO. I'M WRITING A LETTER.
CAN I WATCH?
IF YOU MUST.
Dear Mr. Editor,
I'm a girl 22 years of age but already I've undergone
OO.

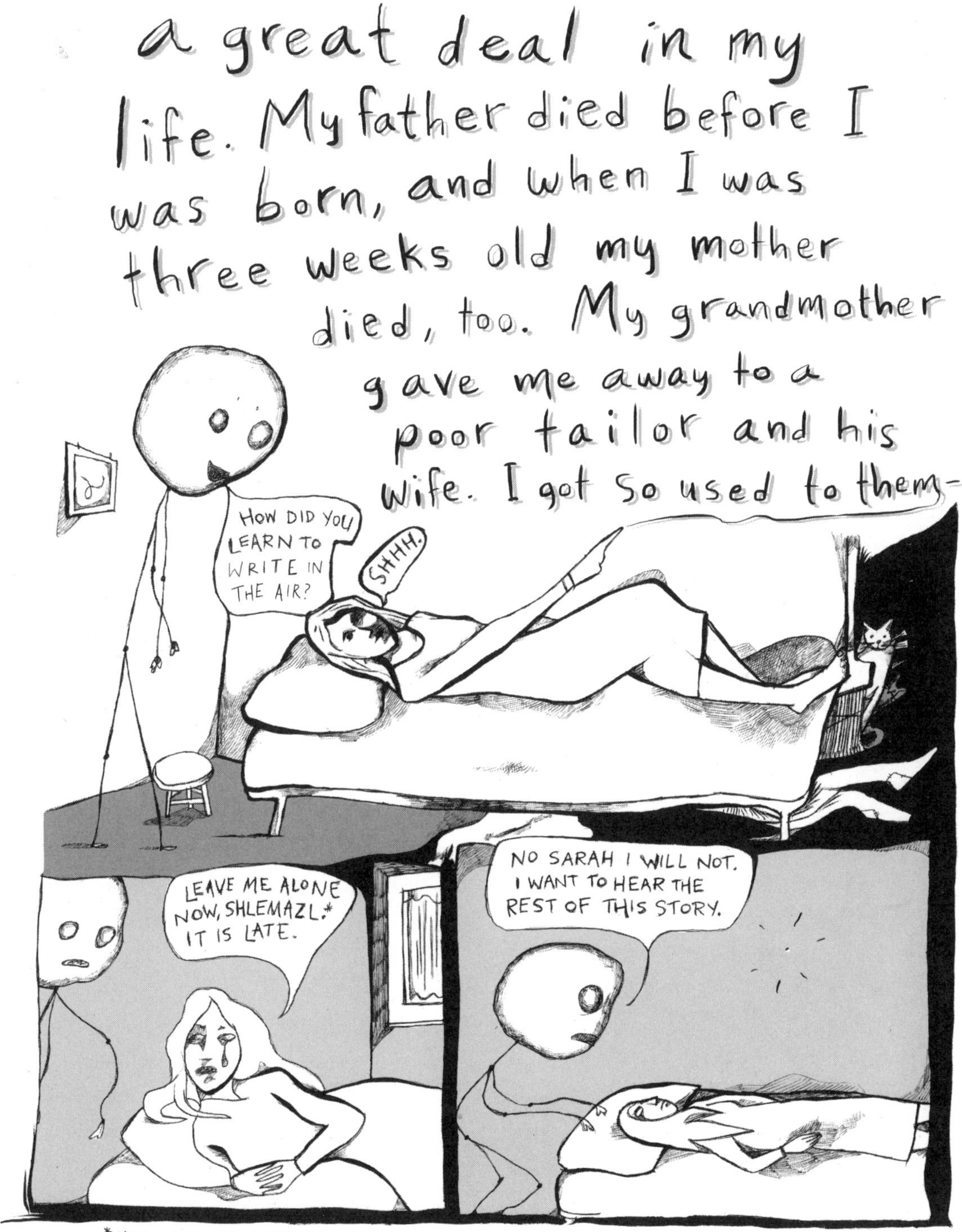
a great deal in my life. My father died before I was born, and when I was three weeks old my mother died, too. My grandmother gave me away to a poor tailor and his wife. I got so used to them-
HOW DID YOU LEARN TO WRITE IN THE AIR?
SHHH.
LEAVE ME ALONE NOW, SHLEMAZL.* IT IS LATE.
NO SARAH I WILL NOT. I WANT TO HEAR THE REST OF THIS STORY.

* YIDDISH FOR "AN UNLUCKY PERSON"

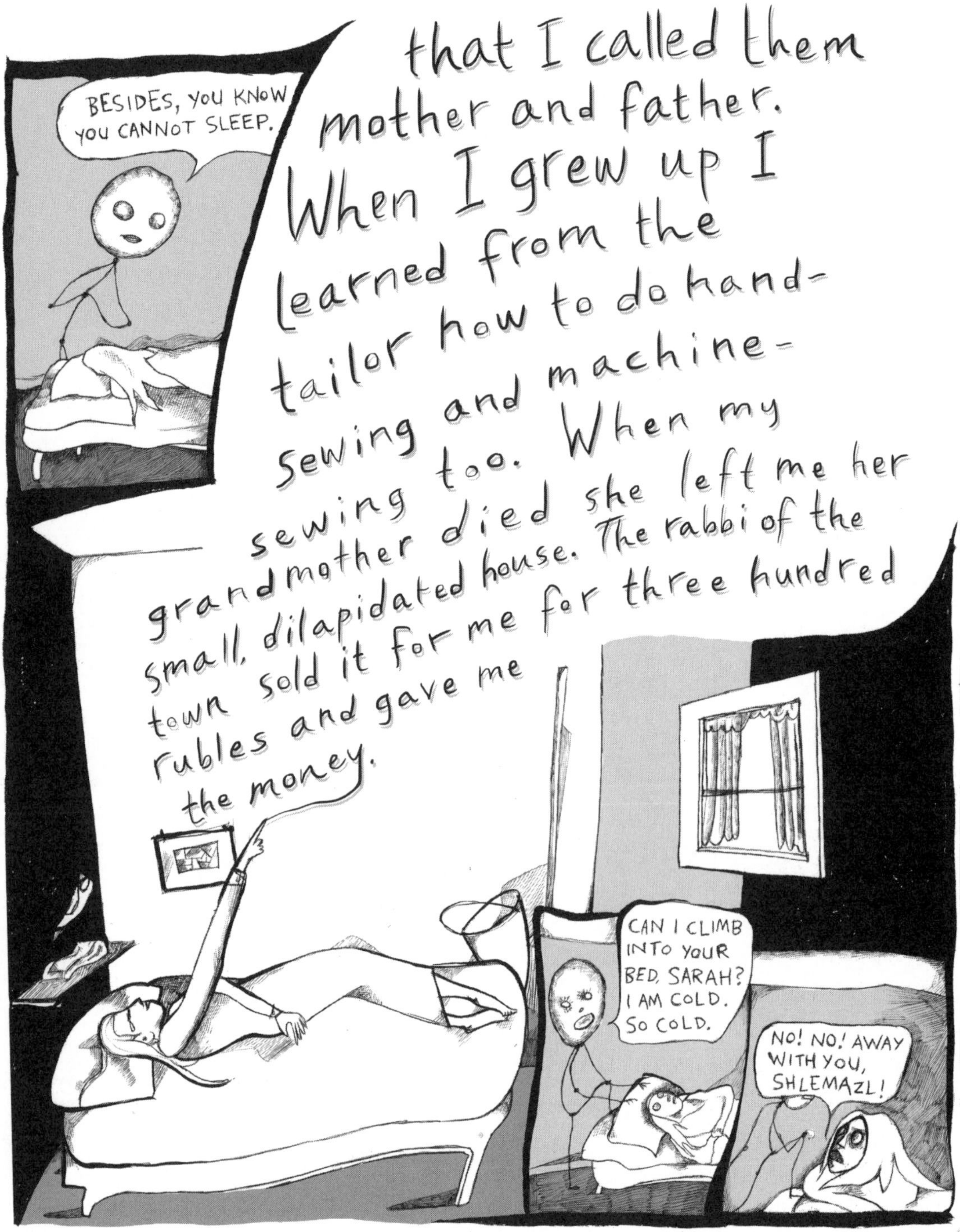
BESIDES, YOU KNOW YOU CANNOT SLEEP.
that I called them mother and father. When I grew up I learned from the tailor how to do hand-sewing and machine-sewing too. When my grandmother died she left me her small, dilapidated house. The rabbi of the town sold it for me for three hundred rubles and gave me the money.
CAN I CLIMB INTO YOUR BED, SARAH? I AM COLD. SO COLD.
NO! NO! AWAY WITH YOU, SHLEMAZL!

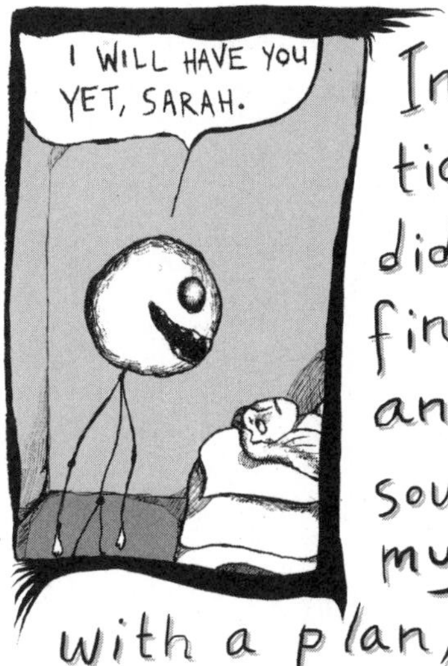
I WILL HAVE YOU YET, SARAH.

In time one of the tailor's apprentices fell in love with me, and I didn't reject his love. He was a fine, honest, quiet young man and we became one body and soul. When I turned seventeen my bridegroom came to me with a plan, that we should go to America, and I agreed. It was hard for me to take leave of the tailor's good family, who had kept me as their own child, and oceans of tears were shed when we parted.

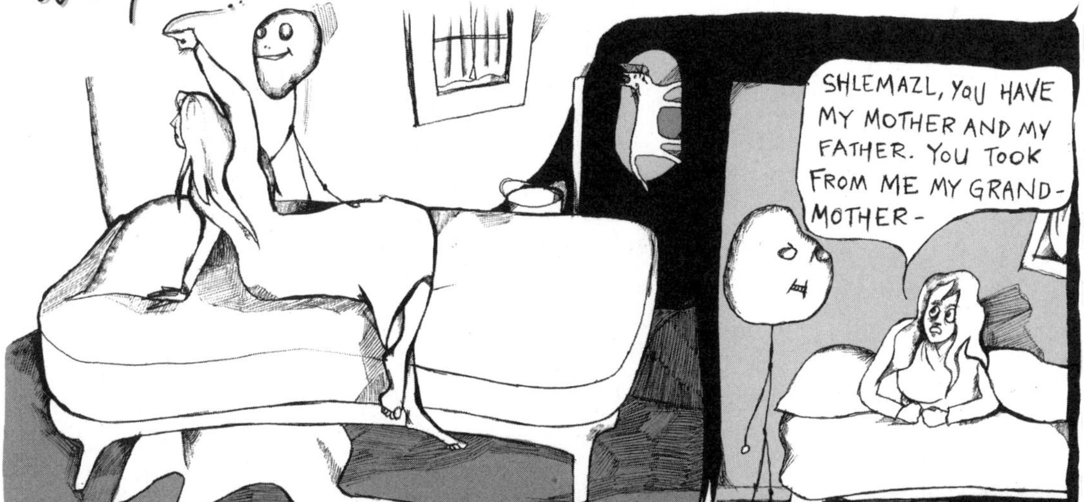
SHLEMAZL, YOU HAVE MY MOTHER AND MY FATHER. YOU TOOK FROM ME MY GRAND-MOTHER-

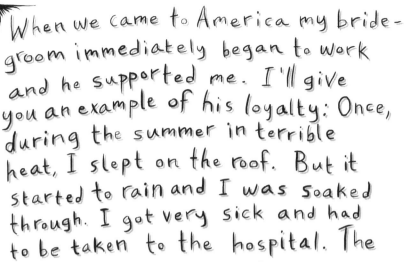

AT LAST YOU REACHED YOUR FINGER DOWN AND YOU TOUCHED MY BELOVED, AND TOOK HIM FROM ME. BUT HE STILL LIVES IN ME. THAT IS WHY I CAN DO THIS:

When we came to America my bride-groom immediately began to work and he supported me. I'll give you an example of his loyalty: Once, during the summer in terrible heat, I slept on the roof. But it started to rain and I was soaked through. I got very sick and had to be taken to the hospital. The doctor said I could be saved only by a blood transfusion. My bridegroom said immediately that he was ready to give me his blood. And so, thanks to him, I survived. In time I went to work in the "famous" Triangle shop. Later my bridegroom also got a job there. Even at work, he wanted to be with me. He told me then, "We will both work hard for a while and then we'll get married. We will save every cent so we'll be able to set up a home and you'll never have to work in a shop again." Thus my good bridegroom mused about the golden future. Then there was that terrible fire that took one hundred and forty-seven young blossoming lives.

ZAP!

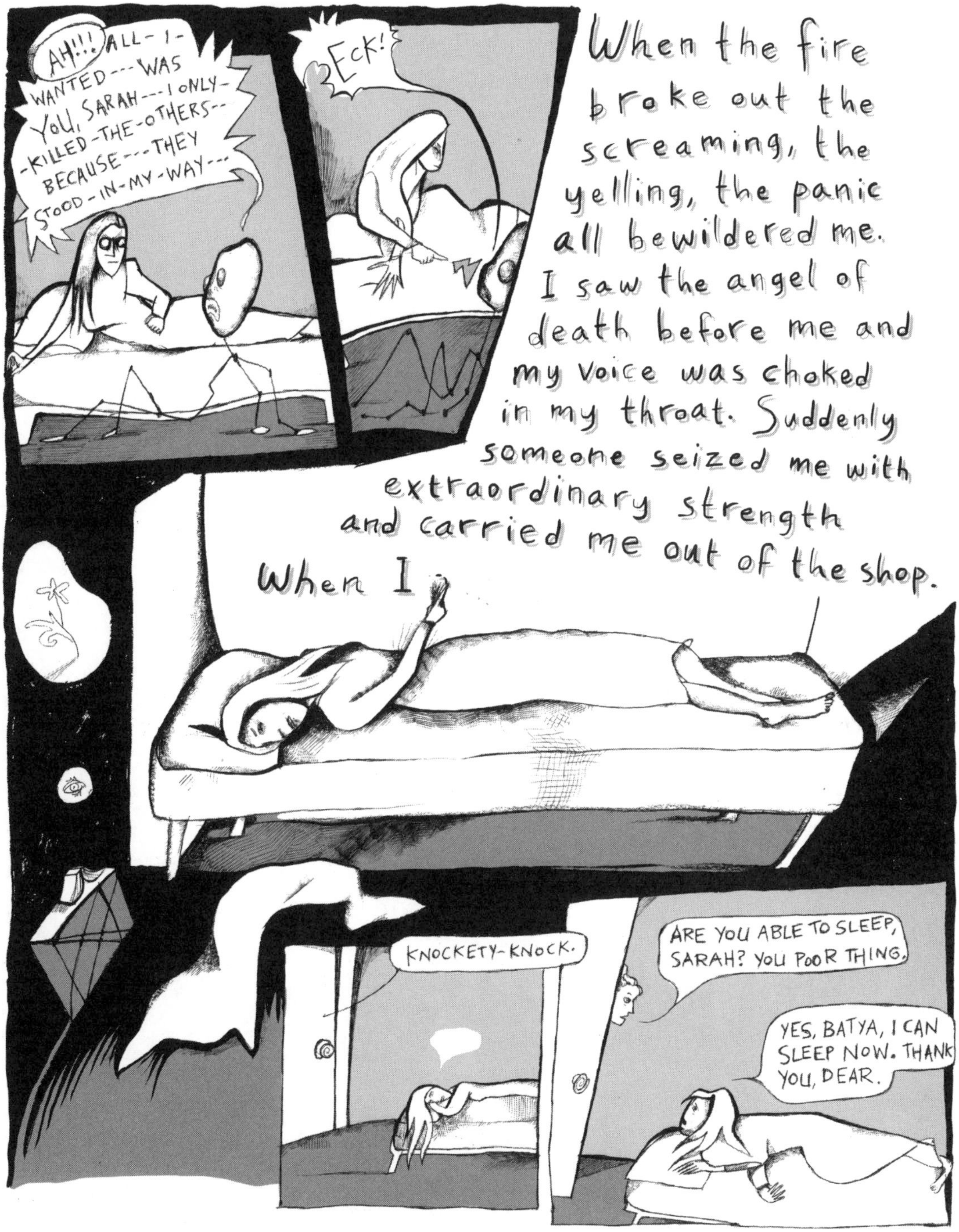
AH!!! ALL - I - WANTED --- WAS YOU, SARAH --- I ONLY - KILLED - THE - OTHERS -- BECAUSE --- THEY STOOD - IN - MY - WAY ---
ECK!
When the fire broke out the screaming, the yelling, the panic all bewildered me. I saw the angel of death before me and my voice was choked in my throat. Suddenly someone seized me with extraordinary strength and carried me out of the shop.
When I ...
KNOCKETY-KNOCK.
ARE YOU ABLE TO SLEEP, SARAH? YOU POOR THING.
YES, BATYA, I CAN SLEEP NOW. THANK YOU, DEAR.

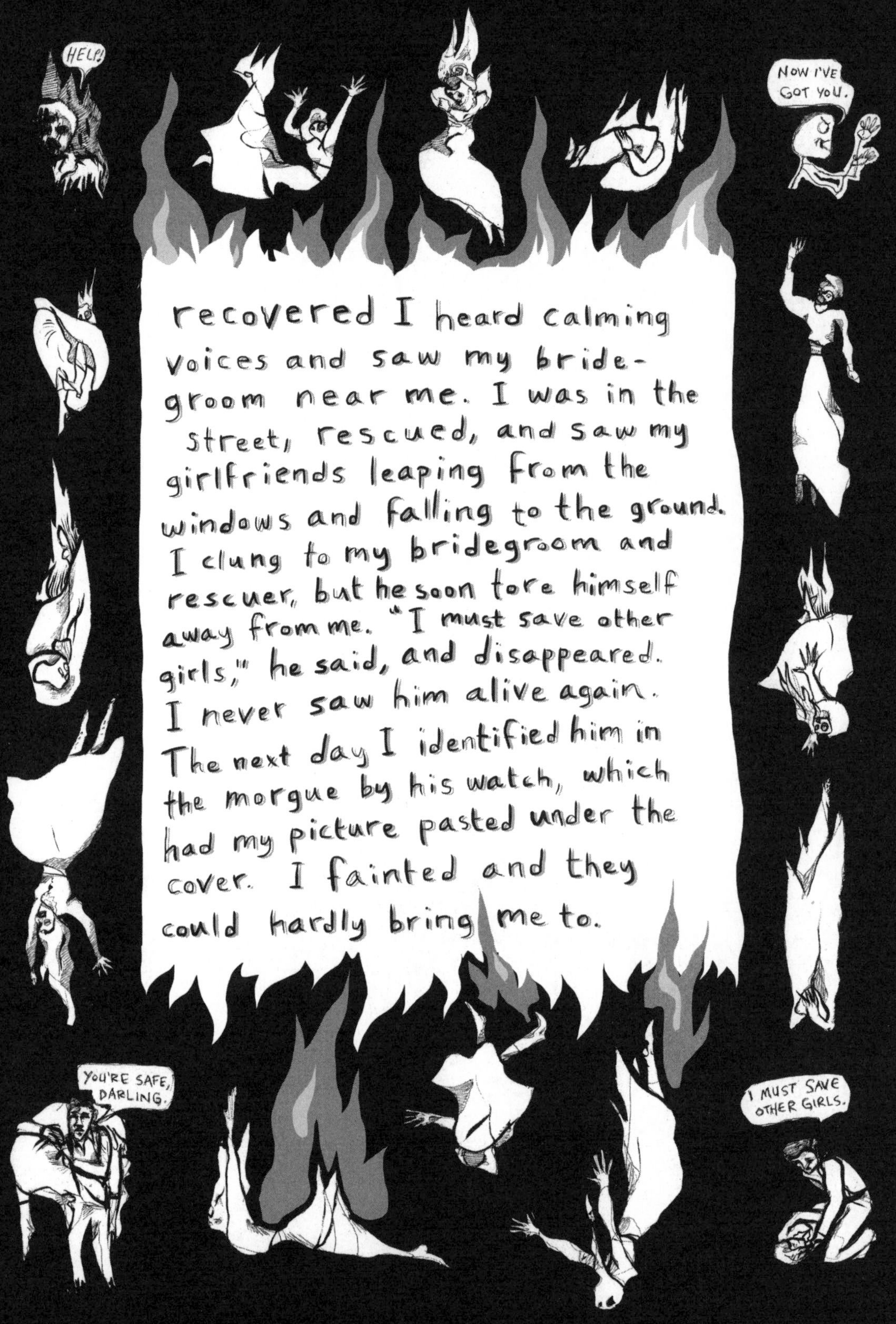
recovered I heard calming
voices and saw my bride-
groom near me. I was in the
street, rescued, and saw my
girlfriends leaping from the
windows and falling to the ground.
I clung to my bridegroom and
rescuer, but he soon tore himself
away from me. "I must save other
girls," he said, and disappeared.
I never saw him alive again.
The next day I identified him in
the morgue by his watch, which
had my picture pasted under the
cover. I fainted and they
could hardly bring me to.
HELP!
NOW I'VE GOT YOU.
YOU'RE SAFE, DARLING.
I MUST SAVE OTHER GIRLS.

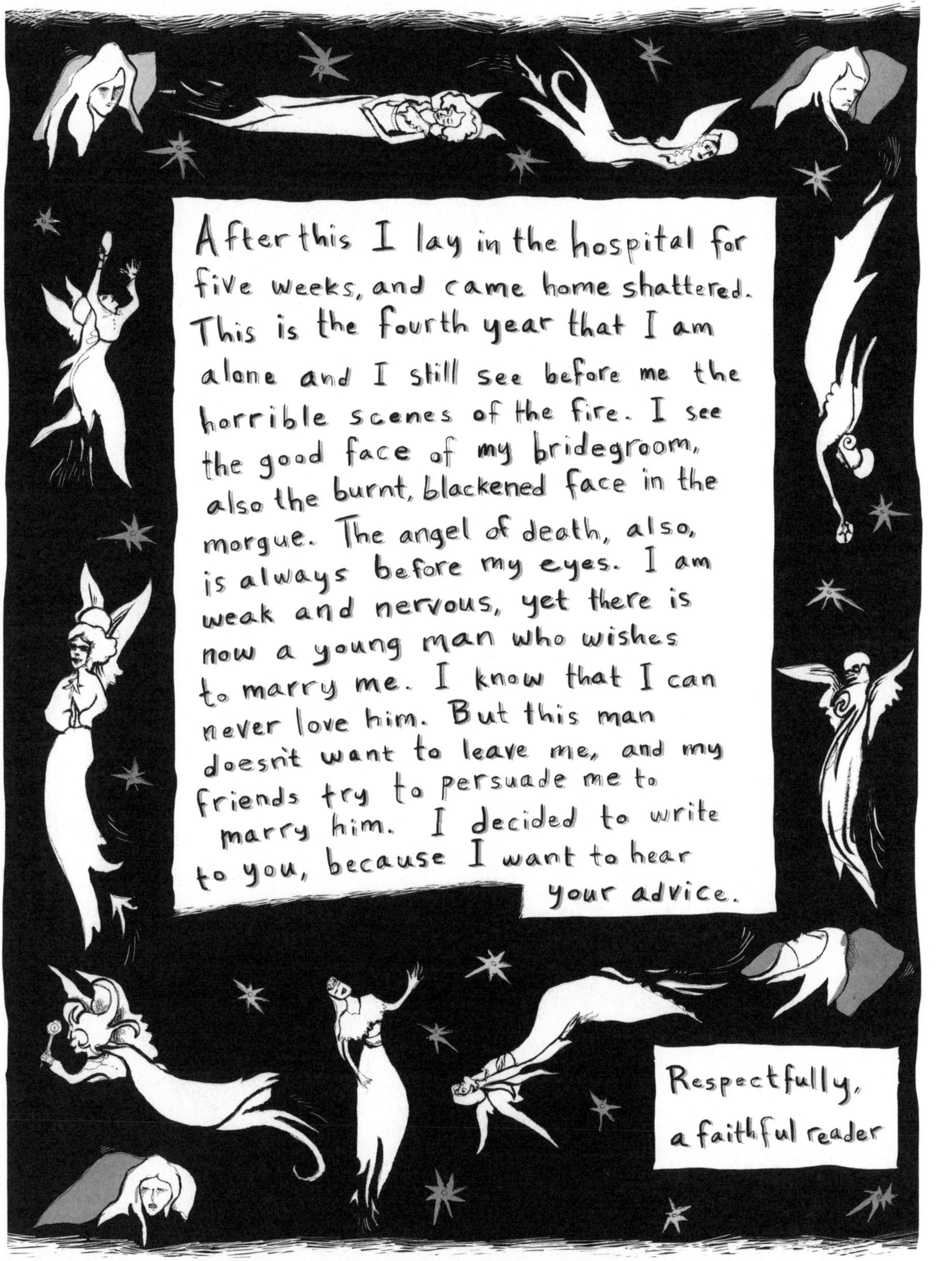
After this I lay in the hospital for five weeks, and came home shattered. This is the fourth year that I am alone and I still see before me the horrible scenes of the fire. I see the good face of my bridegroom, also the burnt, blackened face in the morgue. The angel of death, also, is always before my eyes. I am weak and nervous, yet there is now a young man who wishes to marry me. I know that I can never love him. But this man doesn't want to leave me, and my friends try to persuade me to marry him. I decided to write to you, because I want to hear your advice.
Respectfully,
a faithful reader

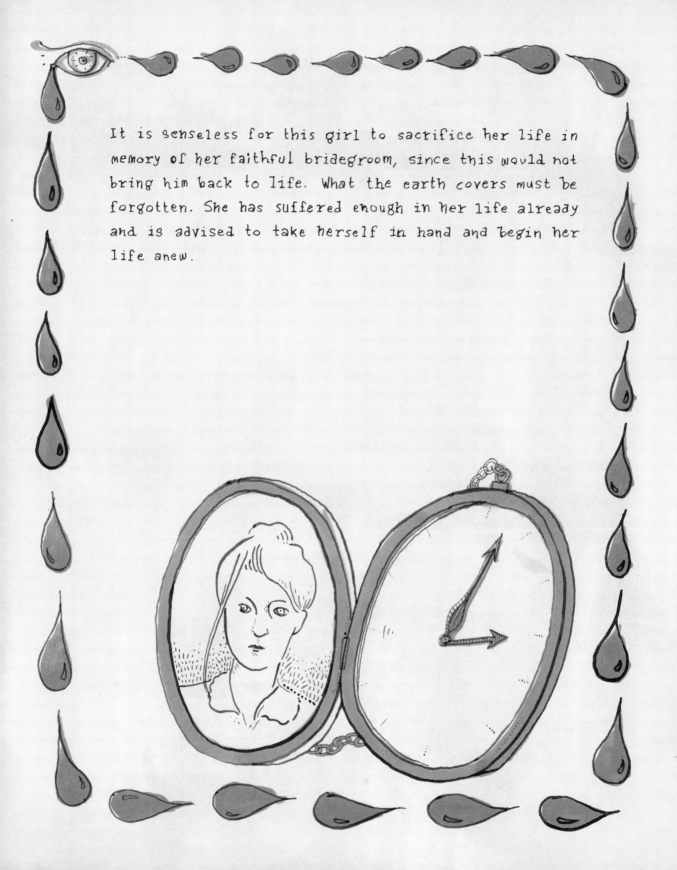

It is senseless for this girl to sacrifice her life in memory of her faithful bridegroom, since this would not bring him back to life. What the earth covers must be forgotten. She has suffered enough in her life already and is advised to take herself in hand and begin her life anew.

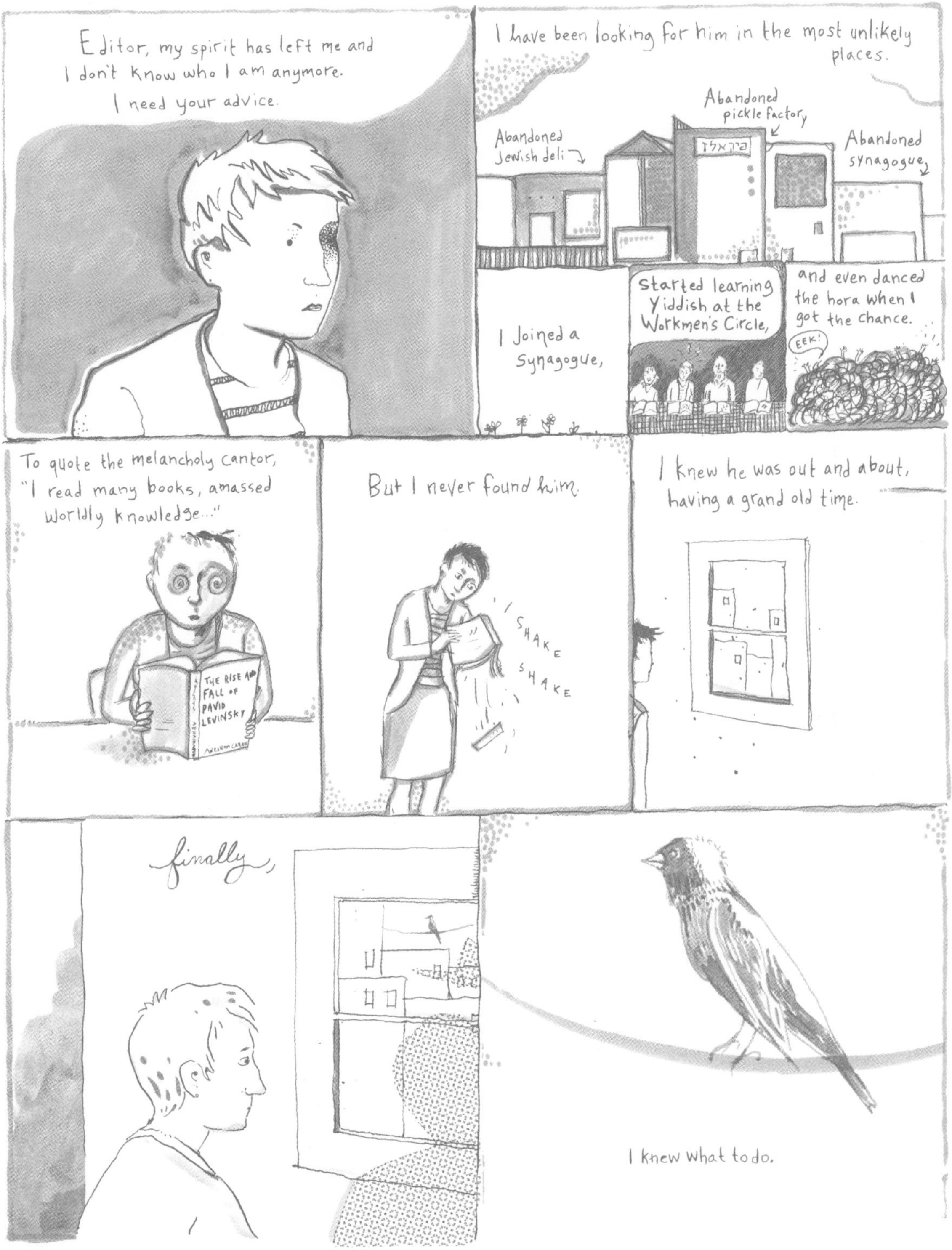
Editor, my spirit has left me and I don't know who I am anymore. I need your advice.
I have been looking for him in the most unlikely places.
Abandoned Jewish deli
Abandoned pickle factory
Abandoned synagogue
I joined a synagogue,
Started learning Yiddish at the Workmen's Circle,
and even danced the hora when I got the chance.
EEK!
To quote the melancholy cantor, "I read many books, amassed worldly knowledge..."
THE RISE AND FALL OF DAVID LEVINSKY
But I never found him.
SHAKE SHAKE
I knew he was out and about, having a grand old time.
finally,
I knew what to do.

EPILOGUE

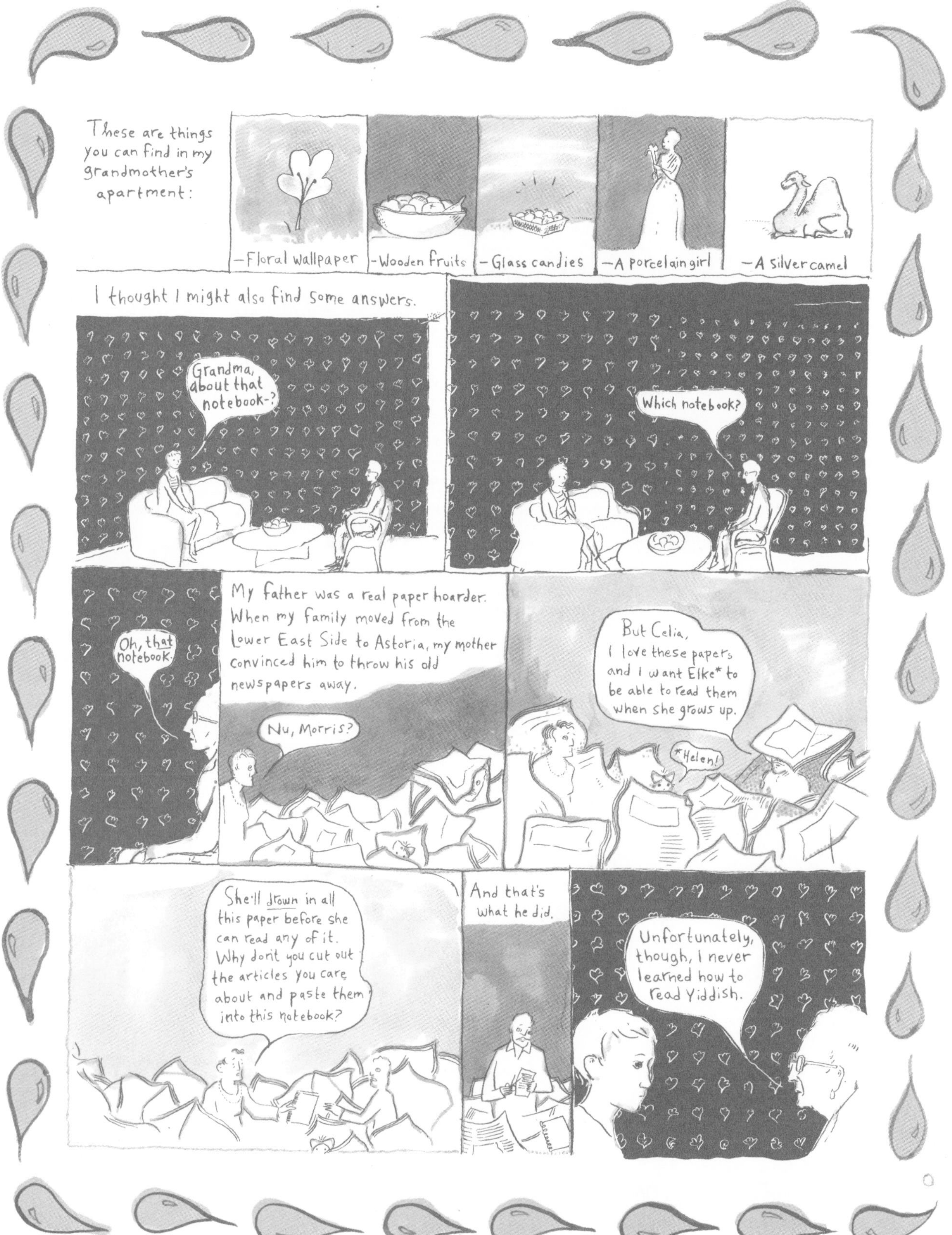
These are things you can find in my grandmother's apartment:
—Floral wallpaper
—Wooden fruits
—Glass candies
—A porcelain girl
—A silver camel
I thought I might also find some answers.
Grandma, about that notebook—?
Which notebook?
Oh, that notebook.
My father was a real paper hoarder. When my family moved from the Lower East Side to Astoria, my mother convinced him to throw his old newspapers away.
Nu, Morris?
But Celia, I love these papers and I want Elke* to be able to read them when she grows up.
*Helen!
She'll drown in all this paper before she can read any of it. Why don't you cut out the articles you care about and paste them into this notebook?
And that's what he did.
Unfortunately, though, I never learned how to read Yiddish.

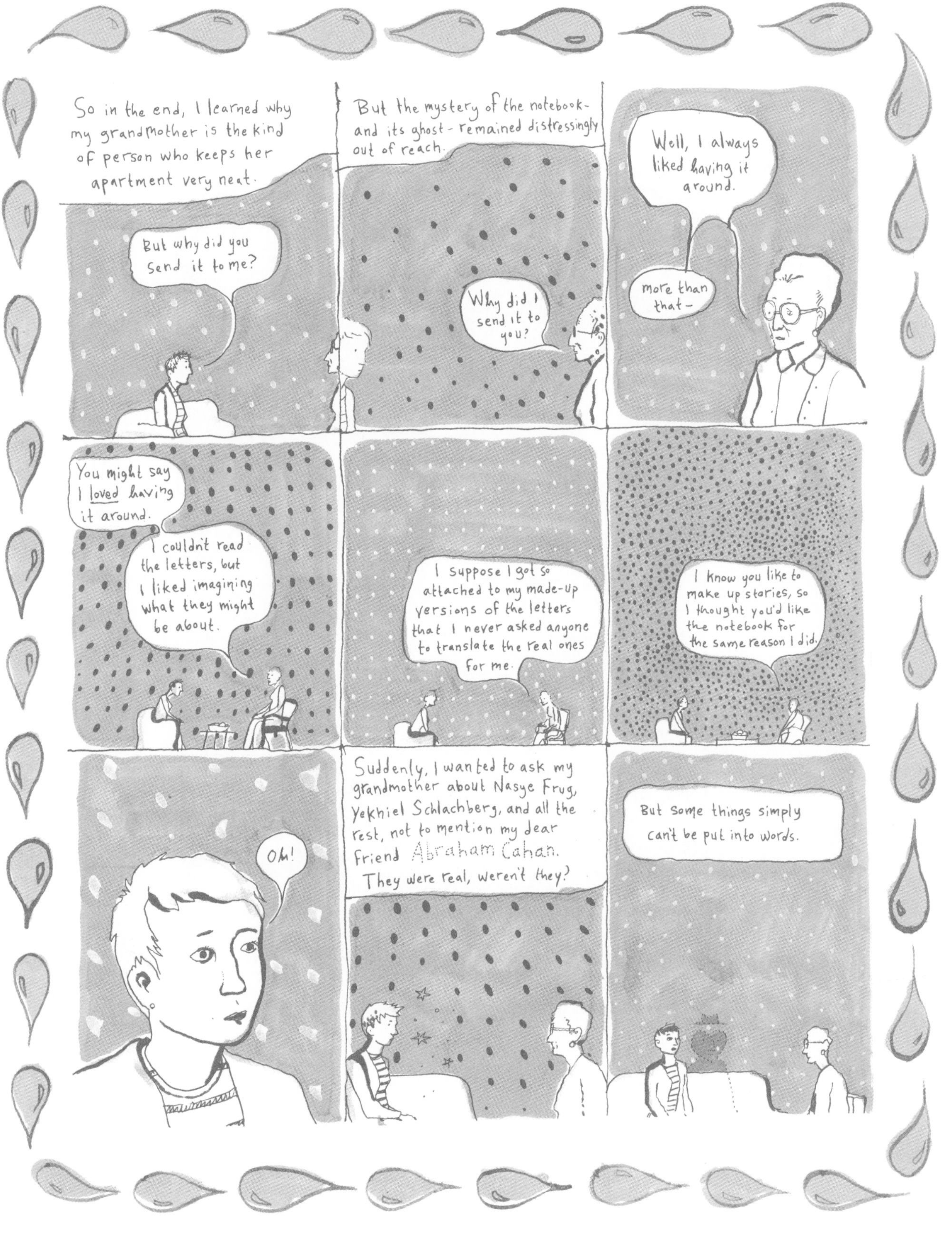
So in the end, I learned why my grandmother is the kind of person who keeps her apartment very neat.
But why did you send it to me?
But the mystery of the notebook - and its ghost - remained distressingly out of reach.
Why did I send it to you?
Well, I always liked having it around.
more than that -
You might say I loved having it around.
I couldn't read the letters, but I liked imagining what they might be about.
I suppose I got so attached to my made-up versions of the letters that I never asked anyone to translate the real ones for me.
I know you like to make up stories, so I thought you'd like the notebook for the same reason I did.
Oh!
Suddenly, I wanted to ask my grandmother about Nasye Frug, Yekhiel Schlachberg, and all the rest, not to mention my dear friend Abraham Cahan. They were real, weren't they?
But some things simply can't be put into words.

AB. CAHAN

AUTHOR'S NOTE

THE YIDDISH NEWSPAPER **THE FORWARD** WAS A LIFELINE FOR JEWISH IMMIGRANTS IN NEW YORK DURING THE FIRST HALF OF THE 1900s. ITS BELOVED ADVICE COLUMN, "A BINTEL BRIEF," WAS INTRODUCED IN 1906 BY THE PAPER'S EDITOR, ABRAHAM CAHAN. THE LETTERS CAHAN RECEIVED FROM HIS READERS WERE FULL OF THE KIND OF RAW DESPERATION AND HOPEFULNESS WE <u>ALL</u> FEEL, UNDER EVERYTHING. THEY ARE TIMELESS.

BRILLIANT, MERCURIAL AND CRANKY, CAHAN WAS A MAJOR FIGURE IN THE NEWSPAPER AND LITERARY WORLDS, AND A FORCE IN THE LABOR MOVEMENT. HIS AUTOBIOGRAPHY, **THE EDUCATION OF ABRAHAM CAHAN** (JEWISH PUBLICATION SOCIETY OF AMERICA, 1969), IS A SECRET AMERICAN CLASSIC. THE TRANSLATED ENGLISH-LANGUAGE COLLECTION OF BINTEL BRIEF LETTERS, **A BINTEL BRIEF: SIXTY YEARS OF LETTERS FROM THE LOWER EAST SIDE TO THE JEWISH DAILY FORWARD**, EDITED BY ISAAC METZKER (DOUBLEDAY, 1971), IS WORTH READING FIVE THOUSAND TIMES. YOU CAN STILL SEE THE ICONIC **FORWARD** BUILDING ON THE LOWER EAST SIDE, ALTHOUGH **THE FORWARD**'S OFFICES ARE NO LONGER THERE.

BECAUSE OF THE TYPE OF STORYTELLING COMICS REQUIRE, THE LETTERS IN THIS BOOK ARE ADAPTATIONS OF THE ORIGINALS, FAITHFUL IN SPIRIT AND STORY ARC, BUT CONDENSED AND EDITED. SIX OF THE LETTERS I ADAPTED IN THIS BOOK— "THE WATCH," "FATHER," "NASYE FRUG," "BORN OUT OF WEDLOCK," "THE TWO-TIMER" AND "A CRIMINAL" —— CAME FROM COPIES OF **THE FORWARD** PUBLISHED IN 1906 AND 1907, PRESERVED ON MICROFILM IN THE NEW YORK PUBLIC LIBRARY. THEY WERE TRANSLATED INTO ENGLISH FOR ME BY JORDAN KUTZIK. THE STORIES "A MAD (?) BARBER," "FORMER ASSISTANT DETECTIVE," "THE BRIDEGROOM," "THE MELANCHOLY CANTOR" AND "A FAITHFUL READER" ARE ADAPTED FROM ISAAC METZKER'S COLLECTION.

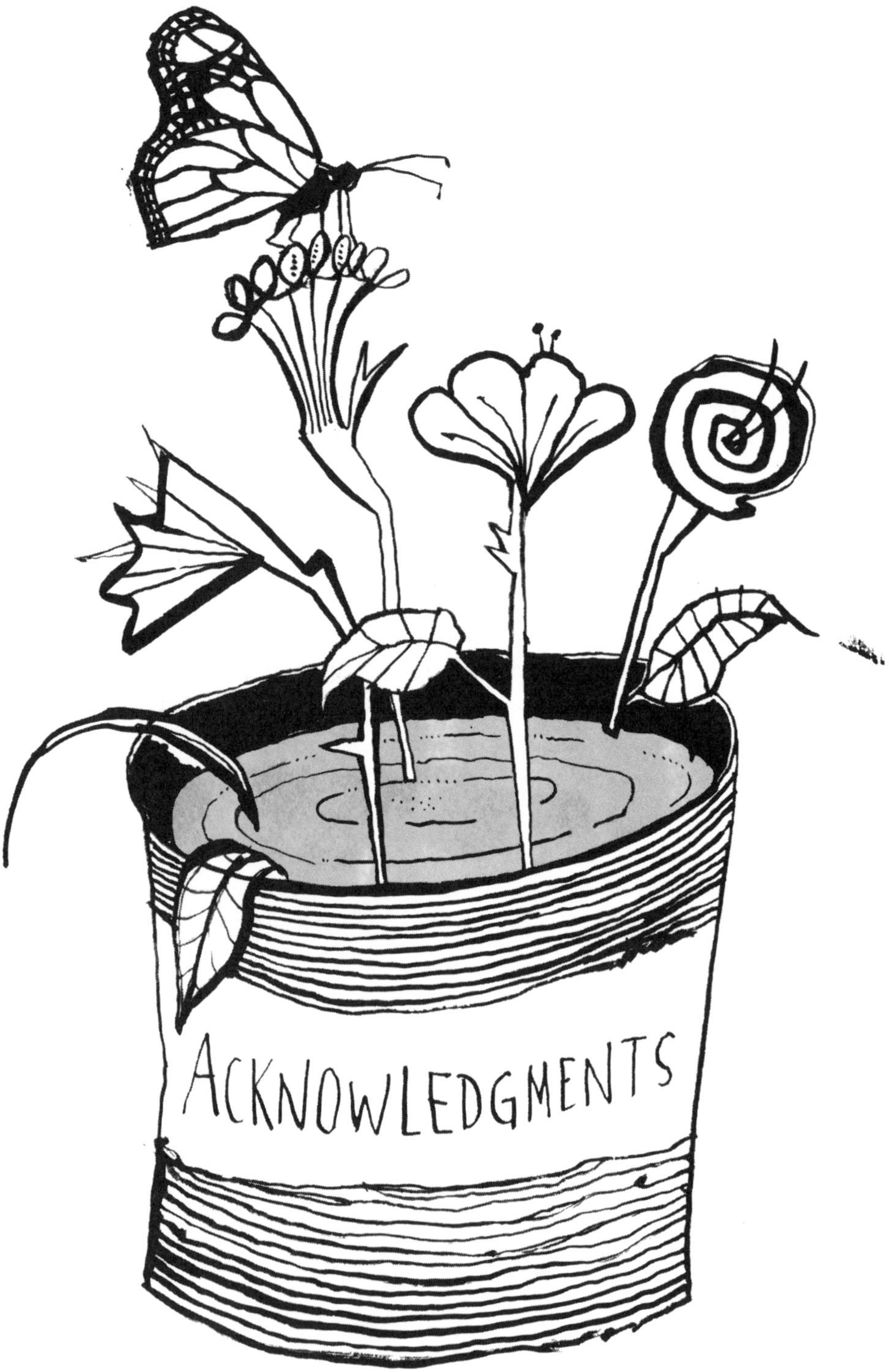
ACKNOWLEDGMENTS

THANK YOU TO HARRIET AND MICHAEL FINCK FOR POINTING ME IN THE
DIRECTION OF THE BINTEL BRIEF LETTERS, TO HELEN FINCK FOR
YOUR BOOK, TO GIDEON FINCK FOR YOUR INPUT, TO TAMAR FRANK FOR
INTRODUCING ME TO ABRAHAM CAHAN IN YOUR CLASS. THANK YOU,
HARRIET FINCK (MOM), FOR YOUR HEART-HEADED DOODLES. ♡

ONE HUNDRED YEARS OF GRATITUDE TO THE SIX POINTS FELLOWSHIP FOR
EMERGING JEWISH ARTISTS (A PARTNERSHIP OF AVODA ARTS, JDUB RECORDS AND
THE FOUNDATION FOR JEWISH CULTURE AND MADE POSSIBLE WITH MAJOR FUNDING FROM
UJA-FEDERATION IN NEW YORK) FOR SUPPORTING THIS PROJECT, TO REBECCA
GUBER, ELISE BERNHARDT, THE STAFF, THE FELLOWS, I COULD SING ODES.

SAMUEL NORICH, PUBLISHER OF **THE JEWISH DAILY FORWARD**, THANK YOU
FOR ALL YOUR INSIGHTS AND ADVICE. MANY THANKS TO **THE FORWARD**
FOR PUBLISHING MY EARLY VERSIONS OF "THE WATCH" AND "NASYE FRUG."
THANK YOU TO THE NEW YORK PUBLIC LIBRARY'S ALLEN ROOM FOR
SHELTERING ME WHILE I WORKED ON THIS. JAY BARKSDALE, THANKS.

THANK YOU, DAVID SMITH, FOR INTRODUCING ME TO FARLEY CHASE.
FARLEY, THANK YOU FOR UNDERSTANDING THIS BOOK BEFORE I
DID — FOR YOUR PATIENCE, KINDNESS, SMARTNESS AND HARD WORK.

LIBBY EDELSON, YOU REALLY ARE MY IDEAL READER. THANK YOU,
ESTEEMED EDITOR, FOR EVERYTHING.

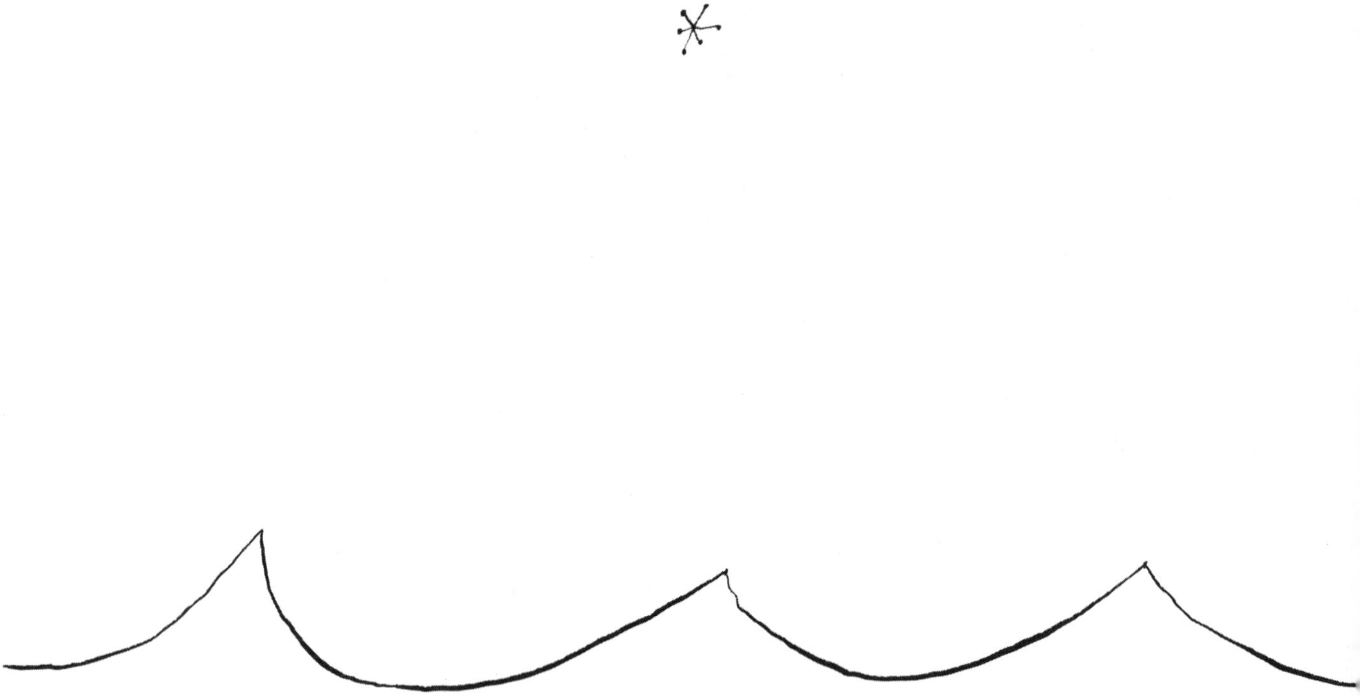